WRISTWATCHES

Series editor: Frédérique Crestin-Billet
Design: Lélie Carnot
Translated from the French by Josephine Bacon, American Pie, London
Copy-editing by Christine Schultz-Touge
Typesetting by Corinne Orde, Special Edition Pre-Press Services, London
Originally published as La Folie des Montres
© 2001 Flammarion, Paris
This English-language edition © 2001 Flammarion

ISBN: 2-08010-621-X
Printed in France

Collectible
WRISTWATCHES

René Pannier

Flammarion

Here, under my shirtsleeve, there is a watch. No, not just any watch—my watch. Like your own watch, no doubt, this one has a history. It was a much anticipated birthday present—I was just twelve years old, and this first watch was the proof that for my parents, I was now an adult, with all the privileges and responsibilities that adulthood brings. No more could I play late with my friends after school, claiming I had lost track of time! My first watch is with me still, all these years later, still reminding me when it is time to return home to those I love.

CONTENTS

Introduction......................*10*

Glossary.............................*31*

I - MECHANICAL
wristwatches....................*34*

II - CHRONOGRAPH
wristwatches.....................*100*

III - DESIGNER
wristwatches...................*158*

IV - PROFESSIONAL
wristwatches.................*214*

V - AUTOMATIC
wristwatches....................................246

VI - ELECTRIC & ELECTRONIC
wristwatches..........................288

VII - COMPLEX
wristwatches....................334

Index....................................372
Addresses & Information..........376

Introduction

Who made the first wristwatch? No one really knows. It may have been a man by the name of Nitot, a Parisian jeweler, who lived in the early nineteenth century. He is said to have created his original design for the wedding of Maximilian-Joseph, King of Bavaria. There are other candidates for this claim to immortality, however. Several biographers of the philosopher and inventor of the calculator, Blaise Pascal, claim that he attached a fob-watch to his wrist, finding this arrangement far more convenient than taking the watch from his vest pocket and examining it twenty times a day.

What does seem certain is that the wristwatch was developed as an extension of the bracelet or bangle, an item of feminine adornment. Jewelers designed the first metal watch-bracelets as women's wear. Hitherto, ladies had worn watches as pins or fobs attached to a delicate chain.

Although it started life as an item of women's finery, the watch-bracelet was subsequently adopted by the military. Historian Guiseppe Grazzani notes that in 1880, the firm of Girard-Perregaux supplied watch-bracelets to senior officers of the German navy. Subsequently, British officers were given the right to wear a wrist-watch on a metal band, but it was not until the First World War that the wearing of a wristwatch came into general use. In battle, it was essential for every officer to be able to tell the time at any given moment—and that time had to be the same for everyone. The hands and the numbers were even painted with a phosphorescent substance so that the time could be read in the dark. A mesh cover,

This unusual silver fob watch has a fan-shaped case with two hands that span an angle of about 100 degrees, then return to the start. The minute hand does so every hour and the hour hand every twelve hours.

could be read in the dark. A mesh cover, sometimes elegantly wrought, was used to protect the glass from damage by projectiles and mud, but the mesh was wide enough to permit the time to be read through it. Thus the first mass-produced watches were worn by ordinary soldiers.

As soon as peace was restored, factory workers, farmers, and office clerks returning to civilian life retained the habit of wearing the timepiece that had been their companion in the trenches—the watch that had accompanied them through so many dark hours.

This was the catalyst needed for the mass manufacture of wristwatches.

The movable grille covering this soldier's watch was designed to protect it from all types of projectiles and shrapnel.

Americans, with their enthusiasm for the new craze of time-and-motion study, adopted the wristwatch eagerly, causing a trade war to break out between American, Swiss, and British watchmakers. The victors were the Swiss watchmakers, whose reputation for quality led them to dominate the market for decades.

Back to the origins of watch-making. Mechanisms gradually improved, and before long, thanks to the anchor escapement, watches were being made that were capable of operating in any position. Shock resistance also improved considerably with the development of traveling clocks. At the same time, miniaturization became possible

1944: American bomber pilots synchronizing their watches during a briefing before they leave on a mission.

and from the sixteenth century onward, timepieces became incorporated into jewelry. Once clockmakers had also overcome problems of accuracy, they were able to pursue their research in even greater depth.

As soon as clocks were able to accommodate additional features, these were applied to watches. The information that watches could now convey included the phases of the moon, the date, the day of the week, along with chimes and bells of all kinds. Since the months of the year are not all of the same length, the mechanism needed to

The sundial is the most primitive way of reading the time, but sundials can still be found all over the world. There are even pocket sundials!

Switzerland became an important watchmaking center at the beginning of the twentieth century. This engraving shows the Longines factory, opened in 1900.

incorporate the notion of months lasting 28, 30, or 31 days—not forgetting leap years. This last complication required watchmakers to mount an additional wheel, within the tiny space available inside a watchcase, that would perform a complete turn only once every four years! Jaeger-LeCoultre was a pioneer in this field.

After it had introduced its Eterna model in 1916, the firm even managed to produce an alarm watch containing a little bell that rang at the chosen time. This feature was adopted much later when Jaeger LeCoultre were among the first to include an alarm feature in their wristwatches. The famous Memovox model, introduced in the 1950s, had separate crowns to be used for rewinding the movement and rewinding the alarm mechanism.

The first stopwatch was invented by an Austrian named Joseph Winnerl in 1831. "The mechanism makes it possible to stop an additional seconds hand, known as the flyback hand, to indicate an intermediate time, while the main seconds hand continues to operate normally," explains historian

This factory at the foot of a pinewood forest housed the firm of Ernest Degoumois, clock and watchmakers. Competition was already fierce between the Swiss and the Americans at that time.

500 Years of Technology

Many inventors have made their contribution to the precision time industry. Here are a few significant dates and names that stand out in the history of timekeeping.

- *1575: The balance wheel is introduced into watchmaking.*
- *1658: Scientist Robert Hooke invents the "straight" balance spring.*
- *1675: Christian Huyghens invents the balance-wheel on an adjustable helical spring.*
- *1676: Daniel Quare introduces the minute hand.*
- *1680: The second hand is introduced.*
- *1750: Watchmakers in America begin production.*
- *1770: Abraham-Louis Perrelet invents the self-winding mechanism.*
- *1801: Abraham-Louis Breguet perfects the vortex.*
- *1832: Creation of Longines and founding of Patek Philippe.*
- *1847: Foundation of the firm of Cartier. Le Coultre (founded 1833) introduces the first watch with a crown-winding mechanism.*
- *1853: The first factory-produced watches are put on sale.*
- *1884: Breitling is launched.*
- *1892: The founding of the firm of Hamilton in Lancaster, Pennsylvania. The first one-dollar watch is sold by Ingersoll.*
- *1919: First patent taken out for a quartz oscillator.*
- *1926: First Seiko wristwatch produced.*
- *1929: Jaeger-LeCoultre manufactures the smallest movement in the world. It weighs in at under one gram.*

- 1931: Rolex invents the "rotor" automatic
  winding system. Le Coultre introduces its classic "reverso" model.
- 1948: First Swiss-made quartz watch
  exhibited at the Swiss Republic
  centenary celebrations.
- 1952: Rolex launches its first diving watch,
  later christened the "submariner."
- 1957: Hamilton makes the first electric
  wristwatch.
- 1965: Omega is officially endorsed by
  NASA.
- 1967: Beta 2 becomes the first analog
  display watch. It beats its mechanical rivals in precision trials held at
  the Neuchâtel Observatory.
- 1968: The first plastic watch, the Flipper
  by Fortis.
- 1982: Launch of the Swatch, priced at
  fifty U.S. dollars.
- 2000: Japanese company Matsucom
  develops the smallest personal
  computer in a wristwatch called
  onHand.

Reinhard Meis. This is the system that is used, for example, to measure the time taken by two race cars that start at exactly the same moment, but reach the finish line at different times.

In 1932, L. G. Breitling invented a mechanism capable of starting and stopping a seconds hand, by pushing the same knob; another knob was used to reset the hand to zero. A stopwatch or chronograph is very different from a chronometer. The term "chronometer" is all too often applied to a stopwatch, a watch with an adjustable seconds hand, but the correct name for such a watch is a chronograph (from the Greek words *graphô*, "describe" and *chronos*, "time"). A chronometer, on the other hand, implies accuracy. In English, a chronometer usually refers to any watch with a detent escapement, whether or not the seconds hand is controllable, but in France and Switzerland it is only used for a timepiece that has passed the tests of an approved astronomical and chronometric observatory. That is why some simple-looking watches, that do not have controllable seconds hands, may nevertheless boast of having been awarded the much-coveted accolade of chronometer.

On the other hand, there are stopwatches (chronographs) that have not passed (or taken) such tests. Much research has been done over the years into how to automate watches. The various types of mechanisms—including cranks, tubular keys, weights, and winding mechanisms—introduced into clocks in the course of their history, led to the idea of a self-winding watch. As early as the 1770s, Abraham-Louis Perrelet invented a portable

This superb watch also functions as a tachymeter. it calculates the speed of travel between two points. For even greater accuracy, it has three dials for measuring speed: one green, one blue, and one red. The hand on the miniature dial on the right indicates which of the larger dials is the one being used for the calculation.

watch that would use its owner's movements in order to rewind itself automatically. The sudden movements of the wearer, that had so recently been a watchmaker's nightmare, now became their ally. Successive improvements were made to the mechanism until, in 1926, thanks to Harwood, self-winding wristwatches first went into mass production. Since the average human moves his or her limbs between 7,000 and 40,000 times a day, what luck that this energy can be harnessed so productively!

Wristwatches took another leap forward thanks to the new post-war inventions. First electricity, then electronics, still in its infancy, inspired the pioneer watchmakers. The U.S. watchmaker Hamilton produced the first electrical-powered watch in 1952, and another American firm, Bulova, invented the Accutron, using an electromagnetic system that could run for a year without rewinding.

The year 1967 was the most momentous in the twentieth-century history of watchmaking. In the fall of that year, the Neuchâtel Observatory, in a peaceful corner of Switzerland, suffered a shock of cataclysmic proportions. This was the year in which the traditional competitors in the chronometer trials first encountered competition from the quartz watch. The quartz watches that were being made in Switzerland and Japan proved

The search for perfection drove watchmakers to create increasingly sophisticated and complex features.

to be up to twelve times more accurate than the best mechanical watches! A significant change had occurred in the world of watchmaking. Hitherto, the value of a watch, apart from the design and materials, lay in the accuracy of the movement. Accuracy and precision improved over the centuries, thanks to painstaking hard work, flashes of genius, and a greater ease in manufacturing miniature parts. The most accurate mechanical watch ever made, produced by Patek Philippe in 1989, contained no fewer than 1,728 parts. Quartz heralded the birth of a movement that did not need balance-wheels,

The advent of quartz made watches both more reliable and less expensive. This was accompanied by a radical change in watch design that reflected the style of the period.

Swatch succeeded in democratizing the watch while creating something that was a minor work of art.

and thus accuracy became much cheaper to achieve since a watch now required a mere one-tenth of the parts it had needed previously.

The French, like the Swiss, had failed to predict such developments. Both nations had been pioneers in the field but had placed too much faith in traditional values. Their watchmaking industries retain much of their prestige, but the bulk of manufacture and trade has today moved elsewhere, often to the Far East.

Yet the first quartz watch had been developed as far back as 1928. European manufacturers were simply too hesitant in embracing the new technology. The young people of the post-war period were delighted to be able to buy inexpensive watches that were accurate, attractive, and could be replaced easily in case of loss or damage.

Of course, such cheap watches could not be passed down to beloved grandchildren, as a precious Reverso or a Longines would be, but in the brave new world of mass production, this no longer seemed quite so important.

Today, the traditional values that inspired the great watchmakers of the past are making something of a comeback, and many watches are passed from generation to generation as precious heirlooms. You may have one at home, nestled in a drawer or jewelry box, to be worn only on the most special of occasions. If you are lucky enough to possess such an item, treasure it carefully, as time will only make it all the more precious.

The first Reverso models made in 1931. This watch is still manufactured in numerous forms and is part of the history of watchmaking.

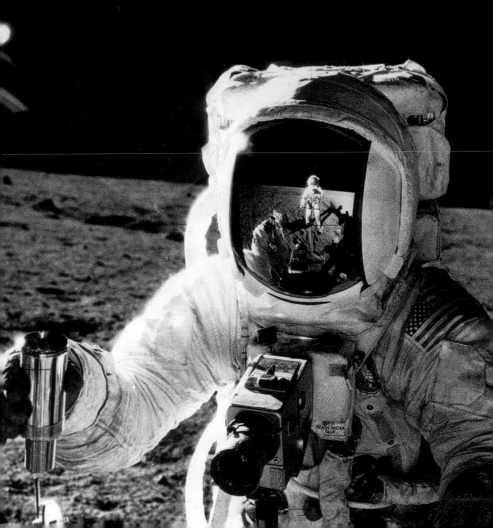

A Glossary of Wristwatch Terms

Automatic watch: a watch whose mainspring is wound by the movements or accelerations of the wearer's arm as a rotor turns and transmits its energy to the spring.

Balance: a moving part, usually circular, oscillating about its axis of rotation. The hairspring coupled to it makes it swing to and fro, dividing time into exactly equal parts.

Bezel: the rim that holds the watch-glass in place.

Crown: knurled knob located on the outside of a watch case and used for winding the mainspring.

Dial: visible part under the watch-glass, indicating "face" or plate of metal or other material, bearing various markings to show, in ordinary watches and clocks, the hours, minutes, and seconds.

The magic of watches is that they not only mark the time in hours, minutes, and seconds but are also milestones of childhood and maturity.

GLOSSARY

Escapement: set of parts (escape wheel, lever, roller) which converts the rotary motion of the train into to-and-fro motion (the balance).

Mainspring: the driving spring of a watch or clock, contained in the barrel.

Movement (or caliber): the winding and setting mechanism, the mainspring, the escapement, the regulating elements of a watch.

Perpetual calendar: a mechanism which controls the date display, taking into consideration months of varying lengths and leap years.

Repeater: watch that strikes the hours by means of a mechanism operated by a push-piece or bolt.

Rotor: half-disc of heavy metal, which is made to rotate inside the case of an automatic watch by the energy produced by the movements of the wearer's arm. Its weight tends always to bring it back to the vertical position.

Tourbillon: mechanism whereby the escapement and the balance rotate around themselves during the oscillation process to compensate the deviations which occur as a result of gravity.

Winding: operation consisting in tightening the mainspring of a watch. This can be done by hand (by means of the crown) or automatically (by means of a rotor, which is caused to swing by the movements of the wearer's arm).

I

MECHANICAL

watches

Manual mechanical watches are those which have to be wound by hand. The maneuver must usually be repeated daily, not because some watches only run for twenty-four hours, but simply to keep up the habit, as otherwise people tend to forget. The morning ritual of grabbing the watch from the night table while still half asleep to wind it up feebly is now almost a thing of the past, as most people nowadays prefer an automatic mechanism. Still, it is a moment that is particularly appreciated by the collector of quality watches.

All mechanical watches serve the same purpose, in the sense that they give the correct time when needed. But the similarities end there, since the diversity of price and sophistication available to the collector covers an extremely wide range.

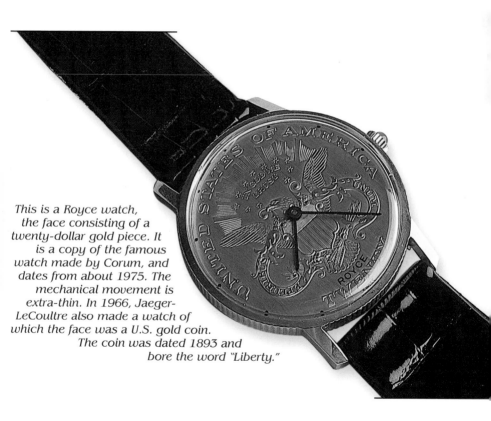

This is a Royce watch, the face consisting of a twenty-dollar gold piece. It is a copy of the famous watch made by Corum, and dates from about 1975. The mechanical movement is extra-thin. In 1966, Jaeger-LeCoultre also made a watch of which the face was a U.S. gold coin. The coin was dated 1893 and bore the word "Liberty."

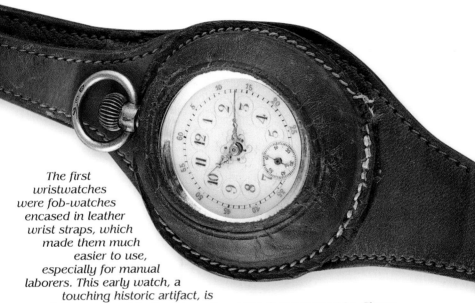

*The first
wristwatches
were fob-watches
encased in leather
wrist straps, which
made them much
easier to use,
especially for manual
laborers. This early watch, a
touching historic artifact, is
carefully preserved in the International Clock Museum at La-Chaux-
de-Fonds, Switzerland. The face has Arabic numerals to indicate the
hours and is enameled, with gold ornamentation. The model was
manufactured in Switzerland by Schild Frères and sold in the United
States by Julien Gallet Co., around 1900.*

Who was president of France in 1917?
Whoever he was, he presented this metal
watch to someone whose name has not
been recorded. Well, in case you were
wondering, the president's name was ...

...Raymond Poincaré. The inscription
reads "Presented by the President of the
Republic, 1917." There is no maker's
mark. That is how a very ordinary
watch can become highly collectible!

This circular sports watch was manufactured by Ebel from 1942 through 1943. It shows the hours, minutes, and seconds. The dial is silvered and there are ten Arabic numerals. The hands have been painted with radium to make them luminous. This watch was sold to the British Royal Air Force for use by pilots.

This cambered rectangular watch with its brown crocodile strap is very typical of Art-Deco style. It was made by Ebel in 1930 and has a silvered dial with luminous numerals and hands.

This circular watch by Ebel is amazingly modern in design. The case and bracelet are of 18-carat yellow gold. In 1936, this watch cost as much as 3,000 Swiss francs. Charles Blum, son of the firm's founder, took over the company in 1932, and made it into a design-led enterprise.

Designers of the sixties turned to squarer designs, fascinated by the attractions of television! This rather elegant watch in gray gold with no visible figures is by the great house of Audemars Piguet.

A modern version of the watch on the facing page. This IronelK, known as a "curvex" watch, is shaped to the wrist so that it can be read while driving, keeping your hand on the steering-wheel. It is mechanical, with a date aperture in the three o'clock position. The dial is navy blue with Arabic numerals.

Actually older than the one on the facing page, this is a "driver's watch" made by Elves, designed to fit snugly on top of the wrist. It would have been the ultimate luxury for an early automobile enthusiast, taking his Grand Tourer, Hispano, or Delage D8 out for a spin.

Reverso, an enduring watch design from Jaeger-LeCoultre. This mechanical model dates from 1931 and is hand-wound, with a subsidiary dial at six o'clock and drop-shaped hands. The bezel was retractable to protect it from shock. It could thus be worn face up or face down—as a watch or as jewelry. An invention of René-Alfred Chauvot.

*Breguet is one of
the greatest makers
of prestige watches.
This modern model
in eighteen-carat gold
has a machined silver
dial with a second dial
at six o'clock. Although
recently made, the watch is
very traditional in design.*

This very elegant excentric shape is asymmetrical, with triangular lugs. It is made by LeCoultre and dates from the 1940s. The mono-metal helical spring movement is by Breguet. The hands are of blued steel, the steel turning blue when a flame is applied to it.

1940s Jaeger watch with a rectangular steel case. Due to its double case, it is known as a waterproof watch. The dial is black with Arabic numerals and a subsidiary seconds hand dial at the six o'clock position. Although less expensive than a Reverso of the same period, the design is almost as attractive.

This is a fourteen-carat-gold LeCoultre watch made in the 1940s. Note the stirrup-shaped lugs joining watch and strap, and the off-center subsidiary dial at six o'clock. The back is beveled. Charles-Antoine Le Coultre (1803–1881) gave his name to the factory he founded at Sentier in the Lac du Joux Valley in French-speaking Switzerland.

A rectangular Jaeger-LeCoultre of the late 1930s or early 1940s. It is a mechanical watch with a beveled back of the case and a so-called railroad dial, a ring around the dial that looks like a railroad track on which the minutes are marked.

This elegant Jaeger-LeCoultre, produced in around 1945, has a delicate red gold curvex case. The lugs, holding the strap, are shaped like vertical water droplets. The dial represents the sun and its rays.

Another rectangular watch, which predates the 1950s, also made by Jaeger-LeCoultre with a curvex case that molds to the shape of the wrist.

This watch dates from the 1960s and has a steel case. Note its unusual black dial with Arabic numerals, and a central seconds hand.

Mechanical Jaeger-LeCoultre dating from the 1940s. The case is made of eighteen-carat red gold. There is a central seconds hand and it has droplet-shaped lugs. The back is beveled. Note the traditional railroad dial.

A classically styled Jaeger-LeCoultre mechanical watch that shows only the numerals 3, 6, 9, and 12. The strap is of saddle-stitched leather. This steel-case watch was made around 1950. Note the subsidiary dial at six o'clock.

An American watch dating from the 1920s with a small subsidiary seconds dial. The watch is marked J. P. Wathier Co., Elgin. Generally, watches of the period had rather narrow straps, but in this case the strap is wide. Note the chromium case, the enamel dial, and the rotating bezel.

This Rolex Oyster, manufactured between 1960 and 1965, shows the date in red numerals on even dates and in black on uneven dates. The back of the steel case is held in place with screws. The Oyster, a name used to symbolize the fact that it was waterproof, was the first major commercial success for Rolex.

A Rolex Oyster Precision watch made from 1960–1965. The originality of the design lies in the strap that is wider than usual, measuring three-quarters of an inch (20 mm) at the seam, although Oyster Precision straps are usually narrower. This is an undated mechanical watch with a central seconds hand.

This steel Rolex has Roman numerals and dates from the 1940s. There is a subsidiary dial at six o'clock that is slightly larger than usual. The Rolex brand became famous for its high quality watches of every type.

A mechanical steel Rolex wristwatch dating from 1945–1950. The black dial has Arabic numerals and an off-center subsidiary seconds dial at six o'clock. The back of the case is beveled.

A mechanical Omega watch of the late 1930s, notable for its handsome dial. This type of wristwatch made Omega's name in the very competitive 1950s market.

The position of the strap on this watch, which leaves a gap between the lugs and the strap, is called "horned." It is an Omega with a gold case made in Switzerland as noted on the dial. It was manufactured around 1965.

This gold Movado watch dates from the 1960s but requires manual rewinding.

An attractive, unbranded watch of the late 1930s or early 1940s. The two-colored dial is very elegant. The subsidiary seconds dial is located off-center at six o'clock.

Large-size Vacheron Constantin watch with a red gold case. The lugs are teardrop-shaped and the back of the case is beveled. The firm of Vacheron Constantin was founded in 1755 by François Constantin, whose motto was "Faire mieux si possible, et c'est toujours possible." [Do better if possible—and it's always possible].

Rolled gold watch made by Émile Péquignet, a talented French watch-maker who began designing watches in the 1970s. This one dates from the early 1980s and is fairly conservative in style, though the dial is two-tone. It has the unusual feature of having a tiny aperture let into the back of the case that displays the movement of the balance-wheel.

This eighteen-carat gold (750 millemes) Breitling is a luxury mechanical watch made in around 1960. The unusual design lies in the so-called solar dial, decorated with delicate rays emanating from the center.

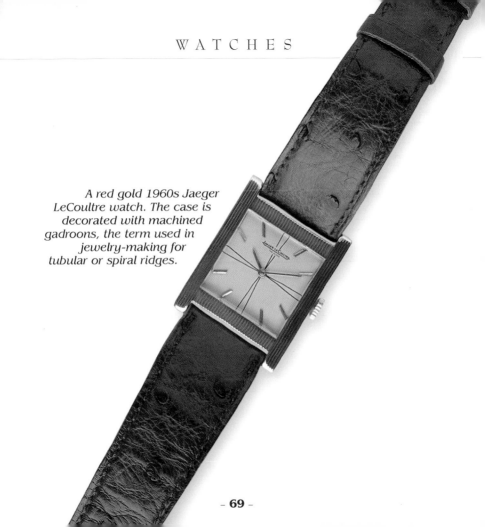

A red gold 1960s Jaeger
LeCoultre watch. The case is
decorated with machined
gadroons, the term used in
jewelry-making for
tubular or spiral ridges.

*Curved eighteen-carat
Cartier gold watch dating
from 1970–1975. The
firm was founded in
1847 by Louis-François
Cartier.*

The Cartier Tortoise watch, an extra-flat model in eighteen-carat yellow gold. This one was made in the 1970s but is a re-issue of an older design. The original was produced in the mid-1920s. The back of the case is held in place with screws and the crown contains a cabochon-cut sapphire. The movement is by Piguet and the hands are of blued steel. The dial, with its Roman numerals, is the original.

Vendôme, a well-known Cartier model. This one is made of gold and dates from the 1960s. The case has a double-gadrooned bezel and the strap is made of tongued leather. The crown is topped with a cabochon-cut sapphire.

This Cartier model in eighteen-carat yellow gold is called the Square and dates from the late 1970s. The winding-knob is topped with a cabochon-cut sapphire.

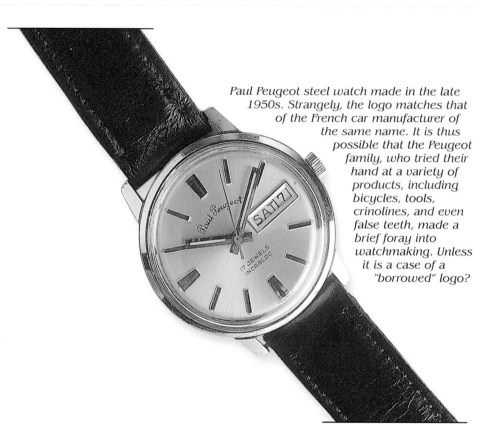

Paul Peugeot steel watch made in the late 1950s. Strangely, the logo matches that of the French car manufacturer of the same name. It is thus possible that the Peugeot family, who tried their hand at a variety of products, including bicycles, tools, crinolines, and even false teeth, made a brief foray into watchmaking. Unless it is a case of a "borrowed" logo?

Rectangular American watch made by Bulova and very typical of the 1950s. Note the elegantly engraved bezel.

Steel Jaeger-LeCoultre watch made around 1945. The dial is very plain, displaying numerals only at six o'clock and twelve o'clock. The aesthetics of the design are timeless, however.

This Art Deco watch was produced in around 1935 by Record Watch, an American firm. The case is made of steel and the movement is mechanical. Note the articulated lugs on the strap.

Sam was a brand name of the French firm Lip, launched between the two world wars. This watch has seen a lot of wear and has a mechanical movement of unknown make. The design is based on that of the watches supplied to the French artillery during World War I.

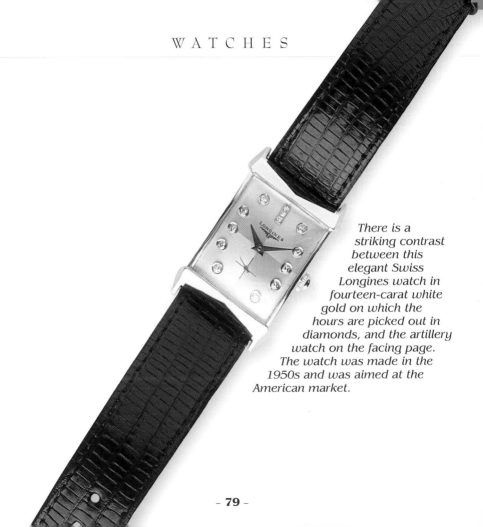

There is a striking contrast between this elegant Swiss Longines watch in fourteen-carat white gold on which the hours are picked out in diamonds, and the artillery watch on the facing page. The watch was made in the 1950s and was aimed at the American market.

This 1930s watch, of unknown make, is of unusual design. The plain dial contains Arabic numerals and the hands are of blued steel. The most surprising feature is that the crown is—most unusually—on the left-hand side. Was this watch designed for left-handers?

The French firm of Lip made a large number of mechanical watches. The model has a T 18 movement and was one of the company's bestsellers. It underwent a number of modifications over the years. This version dates from the 1940s and has a black dial and rolled gold case. The off-center subsidiary seconds dial is at six o'clock. The T 18s were so-called because they were 18 millimeters wide and the T stood for the barrel shape of the magnifying watch-glass, the French word for barrel being tonneau.

The most interesting feature of this 1950s Lip watch is the articulation in the watch lugs. This makes it an unusual model. The dial has a black background and there is a subsidiary dial showing the seconds at six o'clock.

Another Lip watch, this time dating from the 1950s. It has an excentric seconds hand at six o'clock. The watch was a classic first communion gift for many children. The case of this watch is chromium-plated steel, while the model on the facing page has a matte, brushed steel case.

This Lip watch dates from the 1920s or 1930s and has a 22-caliber movement. The case is silver and the dial and raised numerals are of the same metal. Silver combines well with the blued steel hands and black leather strap.

Jewelry of the late 1930s and early 1940s was often large and square. As a result, a number of watches were also designed with square cases. They include this Tavannes model. The name is that of a town in Switzerland, near the great watchmaking center of La Chaux-des-Fonds, where the watch was made by Cyma.

This is a relatively rare Lip model, an
absolutely square watch. It dates
from the 1950s or 1960s. The dial
is marked "chronomètre,"
indicating that the watch had
passed time-keeping tests at a
recognized laboratory.

Another Lip watch, this time a steel one. The model name is Képi and the movement is a T 18. It has a chronometer function and dates from the 1950s, though the exact date cannot be accurately pinpointed. This mechanism is known to have gone out of production in 1956–1957, though watches fitted with it remained in the catalog for several more years.

Specialists agree that watches of the Lip Dauphine series, made in the 1960s, are true collector's items. They typically have a Cupillard 1233 movement and a pierced leather strap. In addition to these red and blue models, there was also one in green. Since then, it has become quite a common fashion for the color of the watch dial to match that of the strap.

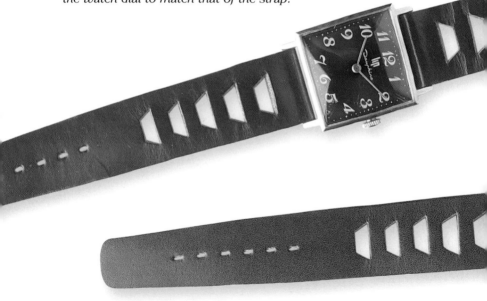

This watch is the same age as the one on the facing page. It was a promotional item produced for French campaigners against nuclear power. The watch is inscribed "Nucléaire? Non merci!" [Nuclear power? No thanks!]. It was made in the 1970s by Lip. The design is supposed to represent an explosion. There was also a green-colored model and both colors were also produced with the slogan in German.

The French firm of Lip had a tough time in the 1970s. During this troubled period, it produced several interesting models, including this limited edition watch made for the French Socialist Party, whose famous red rose is shown just below twelve o'clock. The mechanical movement is a T 13 and the case is chromium-plated.

An extremely rare Patek Phillipe watch of the 1950s. The case is made of eighteen-carat red gold. It is a mechanical watch, the crown being engraved with the cross of Calatrava. Calatrava is a town in Castile, Spain, near Ciudád Réal where a religious order of that name was founded.

In contrast to the elegant and rare Patek Philippe, this Lip watch is much more common. It is a classic example of 1940s style with a chromium-plated case.

A rare and beautiful Cartier watch made of steel, with a beveled back. This mechanical watch, made in Switzerland during the 1940s, contains a large EWC (European Watch Company) movement.

Rectangular Patek Philippe, another very chic watch in eighteen-carat red gold that dates from the early 1940s. The black dial with Roman numerals is the original and the back of the case is beveled.

A very conservatively designed eighteen-carat gold Patek Philippe of the 1940s. It is a mechanical watch with an off-center subsidiary seconds dial at six o'clock. The numerals are Arabic, the back is beveled, and the lugs are teardrop-shaped.

The Calatrava, one of Patek
Philippe's most popular
makes. It is made of
eighteen-carat gold and
dates from the years
1940–1950. There is a
subsidiary seconds dial at
six o'clock. The main dial
is clearly readable
thanks to the thick,
tapering hands. The
back of the case is
beveled.

When Georges Favre-Jacot founded the firm of Zenith in 1865, he knew he needed to invest in the best machine tools in order to optimize production. Thanks to the El Primero movement he invented, his firm was the first to be able to offer the time measured in one tenth of a second. This is a very classic watch of the 1960s with a gold case and leather strap.

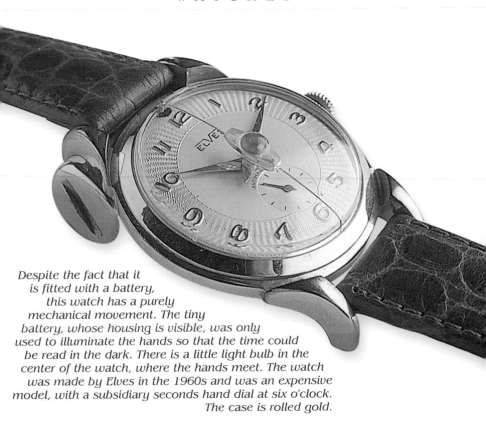

Despite the fact that it
is fitted with a battery,
this watch has a purely
mechanical movement. The tiny
battery, whose housing is visible, was only
used to illuminate the hands so that the time could
be read in the dark. There is a little light bulb in the
center of the watch, where the hands meet. The watch
was made by Elves in the 1960s and was an expensive
model, with a subsidiary seconds hand dial at six o'clock.
The case is rolled gold.

II

CHRONOGRAPH

watches

Many watches can be defined as chronographs, but not all can be classified as chronometers. In English-speaking countries, a chronograph can be any watch with a center seconds hand, but for this book, the European definition has been adopted, whereby a watch can only be called a chronograph if it has passed a series of stiff tests which only a few observatories in the world—for instance, those of Geneva and Neuchâtel in Switzerland and Besançon in France—are qualified to perform. Since 1952, the International Commission for the Coordination of Chronometric Observation has been the body overseeing the tests. It was not until Rolex gained the coveted accolade of a chronograph that it won its world-wide reputation. For example, in 1944, for a Rolex Prince, Kew Laboratory, England, noted a daily variation of a quarter of a second over a period of 45 days. The tests were carried out in three positions at three different temperatures!

Eighteen-carat gold Breitling Premier chronograph dating from the 1950s. It has flat stopwatch buttons and the back of the case is beveled. Note the elegant styling of Breitling's graphics at that period.

Breitling mechanical chronograph of the Copilot type, manufactured in the 1960s. It has three subsidiary dials, a seconds dial at nine o'clock, a minute-counter at three o'clock, and an hour counter at six o'clock. The back of the case is held in place by screws, and the bezel rotates.

Breitling automatic chronograph with two small dials. This is the Chrono-Matic model, manufactured in the late 1960s. Note that the crown is positioned on the left, instead of on the right as is customary. The notched bezel rotates.

Breitling's Chrono-Matic model was one of the first automatic chronograph movements to be manufactured, and it sold in significant numbers. The movement has a micro-rotor and was a standard automatic movement with integrated weight, modified to become the flyback movement used in stopwatches. This watch does not have a separate dial for the seconds as is standard on two-dial chronographs, but merely an hour-dial. The crown is at nine o'clock and there are two stopwatch push-buttons, one at two o'clock and the other at four o'clock.

This Breitling Cosmonaut (1970) has a twenty-four hour dial and movement. It is unusual in that the hands only move around the dial once every twenty-four hours. The watch is extra-large for easier reading, because it was to be used by astronauts in orbit around the Earth. The crown of the watch is on the left-hand side. The case is steel and equipped with an 11-caliber automatic movement fitted with a micro-rotor.

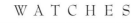

*Twin-dial Pierce
chronograph dating from
the 1940s. The mechanical
movement of this watch, developed
by the manufacturer, has unique
features, since it was made especially for
this model. The black dial has a telemetric
scale that is disproportionately large in
relation to the rest of the watch. There exists
another model with a single-button stopwatch
feature.*

While the Breitling on page 106 has a slide-rule function of a design unique to Breitling, which was mainly used for calculating fuel consumption on an hourly basis, this Cadette chronograph is a much simpler version. The case is of steel, there is a central seconds hand, with a minute dial at twelve o'clock and a permanent seconds hand at six o'clock.

*This 1960s
Breitling is
known as the
Top Time. It is
a twin-dial
chronograph, with a
second dial at nine o'clock
and a minute dial at three
o'clock. The case is rolled
gold, as are the numerals.*

Breitling mechanical watch with steel case dating from the 1960s. There are three subsidiary dials, a seconds dial at nine-o'clock, a minute dial at three o'clock, and an hour dial at six o'clock. The back cover is held on by screws, and the bezel rotates. The main dial is black.

*Lovely Jaeger
chronograph with
eighteen-carat
yellow-gold case, dating
from the 1950s. It is mechanical
and has three subsidiary dials
(minutes at three o'clock, hours at six
o'clock, and seconds at nine o'clock).
The stopwatch buttons are rounded and
the back of the case is beveled.*

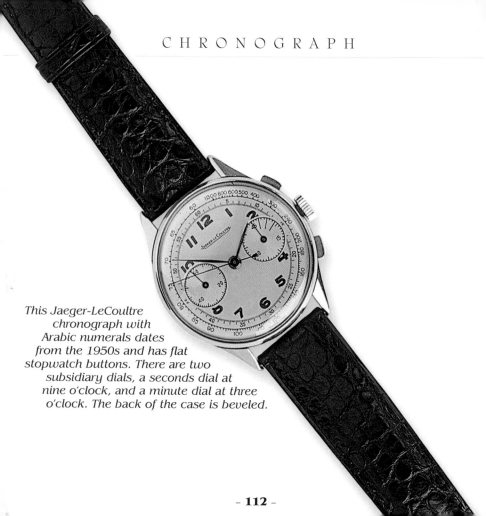

This Jaeger-LeCoultre
chronograph with
Arabic numerals dates
from the 1950s and has flat
stopwatch buttons. There are two
subsidiary dials, a seconds dial at
nine o'clock, and a minute dial at three
o'clock. The back of the case is beveled.

*Mechanical chronograph
in steel by Jaeger with flat
stopwatch buttons. There are two
subsidiary dials, a seconds dial at nine
o'clock and a minute dial at three o'clock.
There are also tachymetric and telemetric
scales. The back cover is held in place with
screws. Like the watch on the facing page, this
watch was sold in the 1950s.*

This rare, twin-dial Jaeger chronograph was made in the late 1940s. The subsidiary seconds dial is at nine o'clock and the minutes dial at three o'clock. The case is made of red gold and steel, and the back of the case is beveled.

Heuer chronograph of the Autavia type whose back cover is held in place by screws. It has three subsidiary dials with a 24-hour rotating bezel that has figures relating to a different time zone, making it possible to display Greenwich Mean Time (GMT) on the black dial.

Both this watch and the one on the facing page are made by Heuer and belong to the Monaco series. The left-hand one is a twin subsidiary dial chronograph. The model was named for Steve McQueen because he wore just such a watch in the film Le Mans, released in 1970. The movement is a Buren Chronomatic 11-caliber that manages to combine, in a single watch-case, a chronograph mechanism and …

...an automatic rewinding movement. Note the unusual position of the crown at nine o'clock and not in the usual three o'clock position. The model on the right, a three subsidiary dial chronograph, is fitted with a Valjoux 7736 mechanical movement. It was made in 1966 in around a thousand copies. The Monaco model was the first square waterproof case to be patented and marketed.

This Heuer Carrera was designed by Jack Heuer and was first marketed in 1963. Heuer was a racing-car enthusiast who based the design of the dial on the style of the dashboard speedometer popular in racing-cars of the period. Thanks to its simplicity and easily readable dial, the design proved enormously popular, and the watch continued to be manufactured until the 1980s. Note the extra-large stopwatch push-buttons, making them easy to operate while wearing gloves.

A handsome and classically styled Heuer chronograph. It dates back to the mid-1950s and has a Valjoux movement. The case is made of gold.

A Type XX Breguet chronograph of the late 1960s, used by the French Air Force from 1954 through 1979. This chronograph, which has a flyback function and three subsidiary dials, was also on sale to civilians. The flyback is a function used frequently by pilots that makes it possible to check successive flight times and changes of course to an accuracy of one-fifth of a second. The watch contains a Valjoux 725 automatic movement. The back cover is held in place by screws.

Breguet chronograph
with flyback function.
This steel aviator watch
dates from the 1960s. The dial
is black and the bezel rotates.
The caliber is a Valjoux 725.

The Porsche design department is headed by one of the sons of Ferry Porsche, founder of the eponymous car company. The Porsche name is so prestigious that it eclipsed that of Orfina, the firm that marketed the watch in the late 1970s. This chronograph is made of anodized steel. The date and day of the week are shown at three o'clock and there are three subsidiary dials for seconds, minutes, and hours.

Porsche Design Chronograph showing the date in an aperture at four o'clock. There are three subsidiary dials indicating the seconds, minutes, and hours. This modern quartz watch has a steel case.

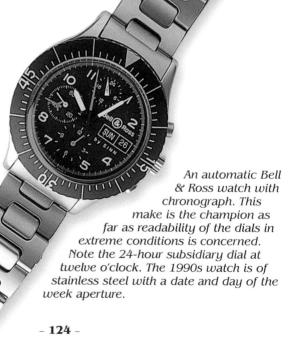

An automatic Bell & Ross watch with chronograph. This make is the champion as far as readability of the dials in extreme conditions is concerned. Note the 24-hour subsidiary dial at twelve o'clock. The 1990s watch is of stainless steel with a date and day of the week aperture.

*Another Bell & Ross
chronograph, also in
stainless steel, with a
subsidiary date dial at three
o'clock and a subsidiary twenty-
four-hour dial at six o'clock.
The mechanism is self-winding.
The main dial is colored black
and the numerals are Arabic.*

Yema Yachtingraf mechanical chronograph made in 1978. The watch was designed specifically for timing yacht regattas and has a small subsidiary dial to show the countdown before the start. The bezel rotates, the case is made of steel with a screw-back cover, and the main dial is black.

This colorful 1970s watch is a Yema chronograph with twin subsidiary dials. The movement is a Valjoux 7734. The watch has a rotating bezel and a tachymetric scale. Yema is a French make created by a Monsieur Belmont in 1948.

This elegant chronograph dates from the late 1950s. It was made by the famous Swiss firm of Omega, founded in 1848.

This Speedmaster model made by Omega dates from the 1970s and has a Lemania 5100 automatic movement. In addition to chronometry of seconds, using a central hand, and of hours, using a separate subsidiary dial located just above six o'clock, the time can be read on a miniature 24-hour dial just below twelve o'clock. The case is made of stainless steel with a screw-down back.

*This sturdy, very masculine watch was made by
Audemars Piguet. The chronograph is waterproof and the
octagonal bezel is held in place by eight screws. The
model is called "off-shore" and has a date aperture at
three o'clock. The case is of a type called Royal Oak and is
made of steel, while the strap is leather.*

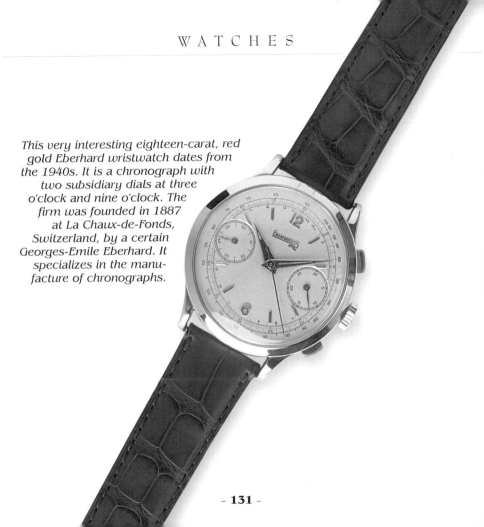

This very interesting eighteen-carat, red gold Eberhard wristwatch dates from the 1940s. It is a chronograph with two subsidiary dials at three o'clock and nine o'clock. The firm was founded in 1887 at La Chaux-de-Fonds, Switzerland, by a certain Georges-Emile Eberhard. It specializes in the manufacture of chronographs.

Miromax chronograph with three subsidiary dials. This watch was made in 1975 and is fitted with a Valjoux 7750 automatic movement. The fixed bezel is engraved with a tachymetric scale. The day of the week and date are indicated in the aperture at three o'clock. The case is made of stainless steel, to which a leather strap is attached. Note the original manufacturer's label, leading to the assumption that the watch was never sold or worn.

In the 1970s, this automatic chronograph with two subsidiary dials at six and twelve o'clock was marketed by the Japanese firm of Seiko. The day and date are also displayed. The case is made of steel with a screw-down back-plate. Seiko chronographs are not very popular in Europe, though there is no valid reason for this. Some collectors prize them highly however, since they are often very well made and intelligently designed.

This chronograph model is called the Pasha, and is allegedly named for a real-life Moroccan pasha or chieftain. It is an electromechanical watch whose chronograph functions use a mechanical movement, but whose hour movement is controlled by a quartz mechanism. It was first made in 1985.

Automobiles and watches have always worked well together. There is proof of this in the shape of this automatic chronograph with three subsidiary dials and a rotating bezel made for Lancia, the Italian sports car manufacturers. The Valjoux 7750 movement is contained in a steel case. The watch also displays the date and day of the week.

This attractive Longines watch, made in 1965, is a more modern version of the prewar "barrel" shape. Note the tachymeter on the bezel that gives an instant reading of speed in kilometers per hour.

Other, less well-known brands
also produced quality
chronometers, such as this
SDH rolled gold example.
The movement and style
are typical of the period
from 1950–1960.

A very rare example of a Bulova chronograph, manufactured in the late 1970s. This automatic American watch is often nicknamed "the parking meter" due to the black shape imprinted on the dial. Note the rather unusual location of the crown (in the center of the bottom lug of the strap) and of the push-buttons which emerge on either side of the strap on the top of the bezel. It has the classic 11-caliber movement.

1970s Préclimax watch of a rather heavy, clumsy design. The movement is a mass-market Valjoux.

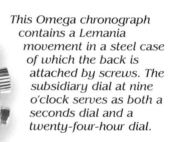

This Omega chronograph contains a Lemania movement in a steel case of which the back is attached by screws. The subsidiary dial at nine o'clock serves as both a seconds dial and a twenty-four-hour dial.

Eighteen-karat gold Omega chronograph, with two subsidiary dials, one for the seconds and one for minutes. It dates from the 1950s.

Recent re-isssue of the Omega Speedmaster of which the first model appeared in 1957. That was in the days before an Omega had landed on the moon (see page 145). Note the triangular hands. If you are looking for an original model, you will discover that they are extremely hard to find.

This 1970s Omega Seamaster chronograph with three subsidiary dials can be separated into two parts. The watch is recessed into a steel bezel on the watchstrap, from which it can be removed entirely, a very unusual design feature.

This Omega Speedmaster acquired the name of Moonwatch. It has three subsidiary dials and is one of the most famous chronographs ever made because it was chosen by NASA for the Apollo mission and was worn by the crew of the Apollo XI, consisting of Neil Armstrong, Buzz Aldrin, and Mike Collins, who landed on the moon on 21 July 1969 at 2:56 A.M. GMT. This version of the Speedmaster has existed since 1963 and is still in the Omega catalog. The model shown here dates from 1967, two years prior to the momentous occasion. Any collector of watches would be proud to hold such a watch in his or her collection.

This waterproof chronograph has three subsidiary dials—for seconds, minutes, and hours—and is made by the Swiss firm of Favre-Leuba. It dates from the years 1965–1968. The case is made of steel and the strap is leather. The black bezel can be rotated.

Chronograph with two subsidiary dials made by Tissot. The model name, Seastar, appears on the black dial. This steel-case watch is typical of the 1970s when it was made. The fixed bezel has a tachymetric scale. Note the two round buttons on each side of the crown that is located at 3:00 P.M. This "star of the seas" has a strap made of sharkskin, a type of leather that is particularly resistant to the ravages of seawater.

The Daytona model is perhaps the most legendary of metal bracelet watches. This Rolex Oyster Cosmograph Daytona is a model that dates from 1970–1980. It is a mechanical watch with a 6263 screw-in stopwatch button. The waterproof steel chronograph is the second generation of its type. The first had the same shape but the stop-watch button did not screw in.

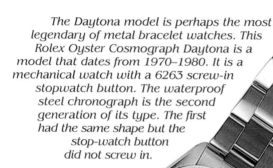

A steel-case chronograph with three subsidiary dials made by the French firm of Ulysse Nardin. This is a 1950s version using the Valjoux 72 movement. It has a rotating bezel, flat stopwatch buttons, and a leather strap. The firm chose an anchor as the brand logo because it supplied chronometers to the French navy.

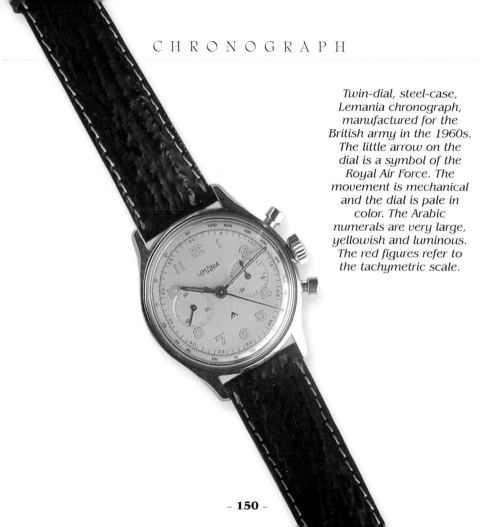

Twin-dial, steel-case, Lemania chronograph, manufactured for the British army in the 1960s. The little arrow on the dial is a symbol of the Royal Air Force. The movement is mechanical and the dial is pale in color. The Arabic numerals are very large, yellowish and luminous. The red figures refer to the tachymetric scale.

This watch was made in 1975 to commemorate the hundred and twenty-fifth birthday of Omega, hence its name, Speedmaster 125. It is a rarity, much sought after by collectors, because only 2,000 copies were made. This self-winding chronograph is certainly not an extra-flat model: just look at the thickness of the case!

Although these two Zenith watches are very different in look and style, they have a lot in common. They were both made in the 1970s and both use the famous El Primero automatic movement (from which they take their names) with its 36,000 vibrations a minute, making it accurate to a tenth of a second.

Both can run for as long as fifty hours without rewinding! Few automatic watches have such a huge reserve of power. This square-case model comes with a blue or black dial, though the black dial is very rare. Note the extremely elongated flat push-buttons on either side of the crown, and the unusual position of the date aperture at four o'clock.

Zenith was strongly influenced by Heuer's La Carrera when it produced this high-quality chronograph, which was extremely successful with automobile racing enthusiasts.

Recent El Primero Zenith chronograph with flyback function (also known as the Taylor function in the 1950s). This means that the center seconds hand can be reset and restarted without using the stopwatch button. It is an aviator watch that, like those on pages 152 and 153, has an automatic El Primero movement.

Modern steel-case Blancpain Flyback, showing the date at six o'clock. It features an automatic movement, screw-back case, and Arabic numerals.

1965 chronograph made by the Swiss firm of Enicar with a Valjoux 72 movement. The black screen possesses three subsidiary dials and a tachymetric scale. The imitation crocodile leather strap is attached to a steel case of which the back is held in place by a bayonet fitting. This is an unusual feature, since most watches have screw-in or clip-fastened backs.

III

DESIGNER

watches

Originally, the most important function of a watch was, of course, to tell the time. This information needed to be as accurate as possible. Once this important stage had been reached, watchmakers next applied themselves to making their creations as resistant as possible, protecting them against the ravages of heat and cold, making them tough and shock-resistant, and constantly adding improvements. Then, when watches had attained a sufficient level of quality, the whole watchmaking industry devoted itself to improving the presentation of its wristwatches, in order to increase sales. Designers were brought in as reinforcements. They introduced into watch- and clock-making a motto dear to the heart of their doyen, watch designer extraordinaire Raymond Lœwy: "Ugliness does not sell!"

Showing the time through an aperture was a trick that had been used for decades by numerous clock- and watchmakers. Yema revamped the style, first produced in 1931. The seconds are displayed in a manner known as "mysterious" in this 1970s watch.

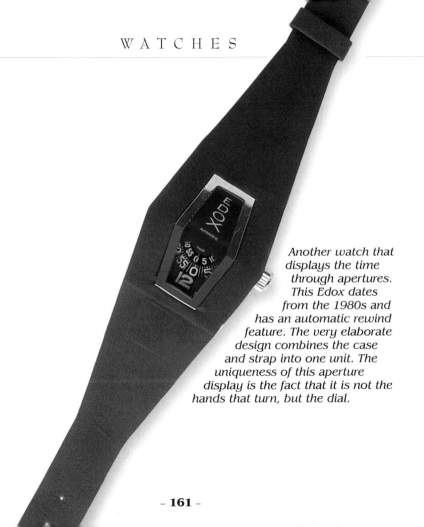

Another watch that displays the time through apertures. This Edox dates from the 1980s and has an automatic rewind feature. The very elaborate design combines the case and strap into one unit. The uniqueness of this aperture display is the fact that it is not the hands that turn, but the dial.

*This Fresard watch
has a simple aperture
display showing the
hours, minutes, and days.
The design and pastel color
scheme are typical of the
1970s. The case is of brushed
steel and the strap is made of
a synthetic material.*

As shown in the previous pages, aperture-display timepieces, first introduced in the early 1930s, were revived in the 1970s. It was during this period that this Famoso watch was made. Its mechanical movement is of the Roscoff type and the case and strap are of plastic. It is a forerunner of the reasonably priced plastic watches that would be made in subsequent years, of which the archetype is the Swatch.

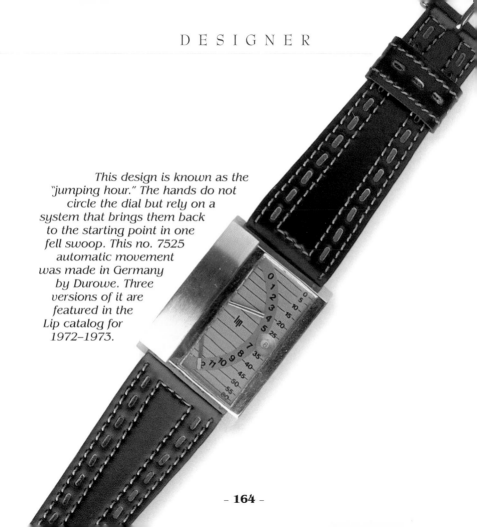

This design is known as the "jumping hour." The hands do not circle the dial but rely on a system that brings them back to the starting point in one fell swoop. This no. 7525 automatic movement was made in Germany by Durowe. Three versions of it are featured in the Lip catalog for 1972–1973.

The first Lip model with a linear dial is shown on the facing page. This second model has a circular dial. The third model, first marketed in 1972, was rectangular, but horizontal rather than vertical. The price tag reads 380 French francs.

This amusing Sicura watch has an electrically powered movement that can be seen through an aperture. The style with its pierced blue plastic strap, is typical of the 1970s, and ...

... has come right back into fashion. But the potential wearer should be aware that the watch requires two batteries, one of them just to illuminate the dial.

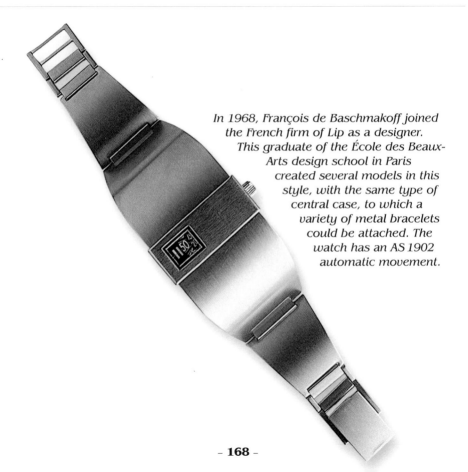

In 1968, François de Baschmakoff joined the French firm of Lip as a designer. This graduate of the École des Beaux-Arts design school in Paris created several models in this style, with the same type of central case, to which a variety of metal bracelets could be attached. The watch has an AS 1902 automatic movement.

*This rolled gold Jaz watch is the Derby model that
dates from the 1970s. It is an aperture display model
with a cap-type case. The crown is hidden at the back.
Three black plastic revolving drums show the hours,
minutes, and seconds. The electronic movement is
based on Léon Hatot's patent taken out in 1953.*

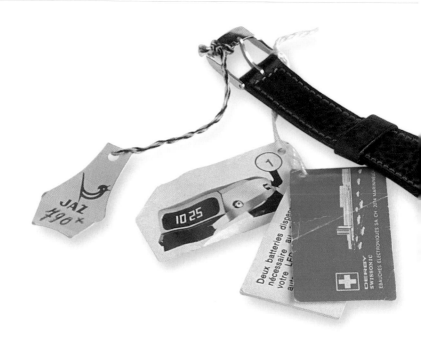

With all its labels, this watch is in perfect condition, right out of its box, and dates from 1975. It is a Jaz quartz watch with an LED (Light Electric Diode) display, an example of one of the first quartz watches to experiment with an entirely static digital display.

A 1935 Ralco aperture-display wristwatch. The case curves slightly in order to hug the wrist. The mechanical movement with manual rewind is fitted with fifteen rubies and a self-compensating flat mono-metal mainspring.

Rectangular watch with a red gold case and apertures displaying the hours (top) and minutes (bottom). It was made in 1931.

One of a series of watches designed by Michel Boyer in 1974, and entitled "The Seasons." This model represents summer. There is a pink model representing spring, yellow for the fall, and blue for winter. These watches, made by the French firm of Lip and fitted with a T13 mechanical movement, are relatively hard to find. They were sold for 140 French francs, and this was considered to be such a low price that they were not thought worth keeping or repairing.

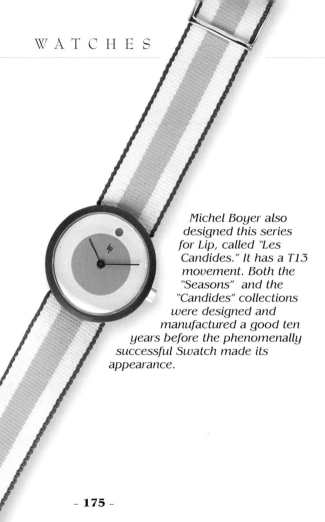

Michel Boyer also designed this series for Lip, called "Les Candides." It has a T13 movement. Both the "Seasons" and the "Candides" collections were designed and manufactured a good ten years before the phenomenally successful Swatch made its appearance.

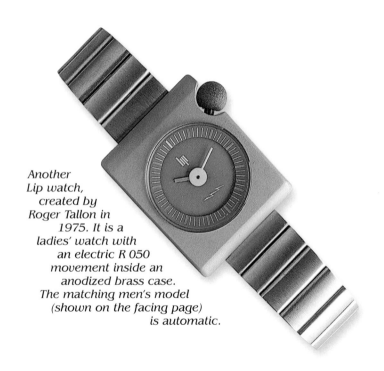

Another
Lip watch,
created by
Roger Tallon in
1975. It is a
ladies' watch with
an electric R 050
movement inside an
anodized brass case.
The matching men's model
(shown on the facing page)
is automatic.

The names of
Tallon (who also
designed the TGV,
the French high-
speed train) and Lip,
the French watchmaker,
are intimately linked. The
designer helped the firm to
revive its flagging fortunes.
These elegant ladies' and men's
watches are sculptured works
of art, worn on wrists all over the
world from 1975 onward.

This mechanical Lip chronograph, called Mach 2000,
dates from 1974 and is
another of Roger Tallon's
creations. It has a 7734
Valjoux movement and an
anodized alloy case. The
knobs on the push-
buttons are black here, but
there is another model with
colored buttons.

A Lip Mach 2000 quartz model that closely resembles the watch on the facing page, except that it also indicates the phases of the moon. It is a prototype, designed in 1989 by Roger Tallon. Fitted with a PUW movement, it was never sold commercially.

*In 1974, Lip's
creativity was
remarkable. This
watch, with its T13
movement, was designed
by Michael Kinn.*

This thermometer watch, with its very unusual bezel, was never marketed in the version shown here. It dates from the late 1960s and has a German Durowe 45 movement.

An extraordinary model with its asymmetrical case that was sold as part of the Cosmique collection and dates from 1962. This is a rare, rolled gold version. The watch (the crown shown in the picture is not the original) is fitted with a Peseux 320 Swiss mechanical movement.

Collectors have nicknamed this watch "the television," for obvious reasons. It has the unusual feature of showing the day and date thanks to a calendar at the bottom of the dial. Manufactured in 1972 and 1973 by Lip, the watch was made with a steel or rolled gold case—a model very sought after by collectors.

Isabelle Hebey studied psychology before devoting herself to industrial design. After working on the interior design of the Anglo-French Concorde and Airbus airplanes, she worked for Lip from 1973. She created this rolled gold watch with its T 13 Lip movement in 1976.

A variation on the same design theme, also by Isabelle Hebey. It was created in the same year as the watch on the facing page. This time, the case treatment is in unpolished chromium-plated brass. The dial, with its twelve black spots representing the hours, is of the utmost simplicity.

This Lip watch belongs to the Skipper series, first produced in 1975. The steel case contains a Lip T 13 movement. The hours are written in French. It was manufactured for a German distributor named Dugena.

Another Lip watch, designed by Roger Tallon in 1976. The anodized brass case has an R 052 electric movement and the crown is located at twelve o'clock, a most unusual position. The strap is a continuous strip of leather, to which the case is attached by four screws.

The great French couturier, Pierre Cardin, who initiated the unisex style, created a large number of watches, including these with their elegant contours that date from the 1970s. This model has an FE 68 movement.

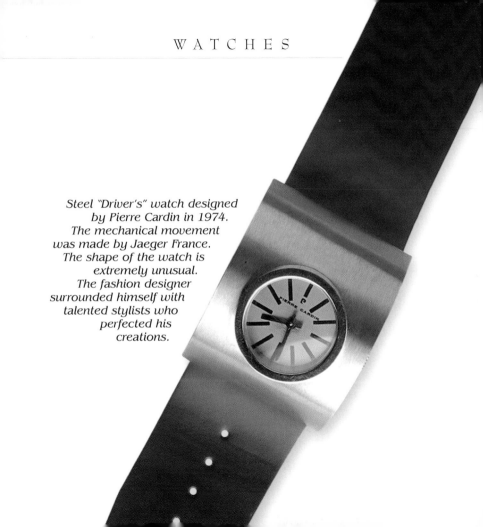

Steel "Driver's" watch designed by Pierre Cardin in 1974. The mechanical movement was made by Jaeger France. The shape of the watch is extremely unusual. The fashion designer surrounded himself with talented stylists who perfected his creations.

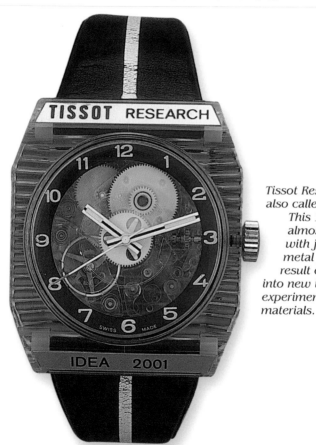

Tissot Research Idea 2001, also called the Astrolon.
This 1971 model is made almost entirely of plastic, with just a few moving metal parts. It was the result of extensive research into new technologies and experimentation with new materials.

*Tissot Research
Idea 2001.
This model was
developed by
Tissot as an
inexpensive design,
since all the gear
wheels are made of
plastic. Unfortunately, the
watch proved to be
insufficiently accurate, and was
a marketing disaster that nearly
jeopardized the brand's future.*

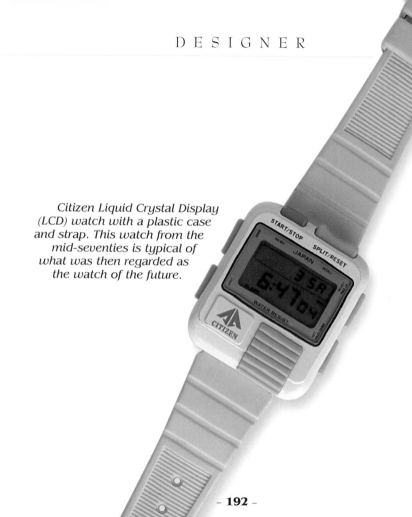

Citizen Liquid Crystal Display (LCD) watch with a plastic case and strap. This watch from the mid-seventies is typical of what was then regarded as the watch of the future.

1972 Spaceman watch created by André Le Marquand, a Swiss designer. Le Marquand was inspired by the shape of the helmets of the American astronauts who landed on the moon in July 1969. This automatic watch was marketed under different brand names, including Tressa Lux. The crown and bezel are chromium-plated steel and the strap is made of Corfam, a plastic material developed by Du Pont. The watch was so popular that 150,000 of them were sold!

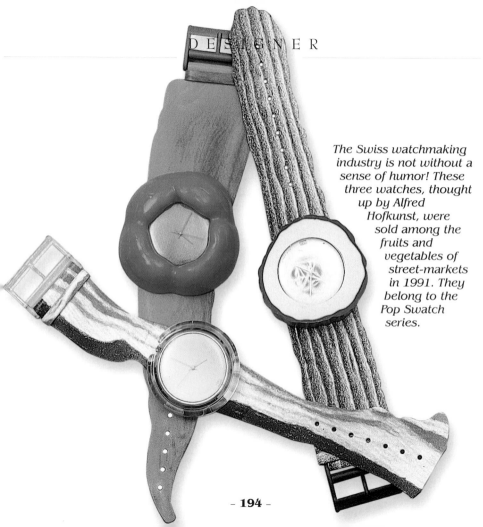

The Swiss watchmaking industry is not without a sense of humor! These three watches, thought up by Alfred Hofkunst, were sold among the fruits and vegetables of street-markets in 1991. They belong to the Pop Swatch series.

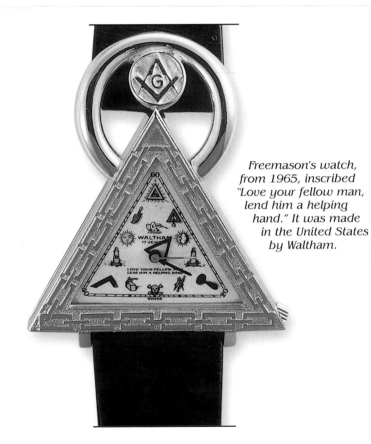

Freemason's watch, from 1965, inscribed "Love your fellow man, lend him a helping hand." It was made in the United States by Waltham.

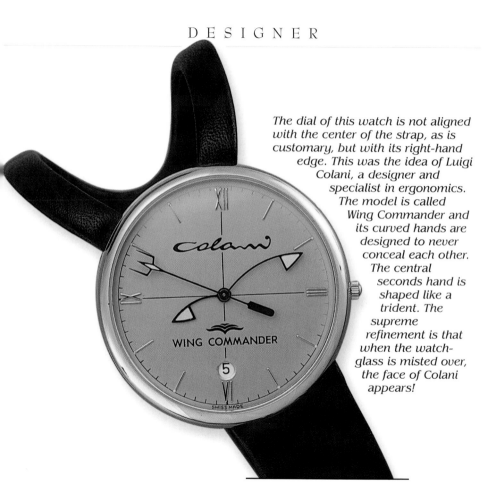

The dial of this watch is not aligned with the center of the strap, as is customary, but with its right-hand edge. This was the idea of Luigi Colani, a designer and specialist in ergonomics. The model is called Wing Commander and its curved hands are designed to never conceal each other. The central seconds hand is shaped like a trident. The supreme refinement is that when the watch-glass is misted over, the face of Colani appears!

The original feature of this 1976 Buckingham watch by Corum is that the dial is made with a real peacock feather. The crown is topped by a sapphire, and the mechanical movement is based on a three-position balance-wheel.

Rolex diver's model dating from the early 1960s. It is a classic designer watch with an expandable bracelet in the same two metals—gold and steel—as the case. In 1953, the French undersea explorer, Professor Piccard, had taken a watch of this type down to a depth of more than 3,000 meters beneath the waves in his bathyscaph. Later, the watch was placed on the outside of the submersible, and reached a depth of 10,908 meters without sustaining any damage.

The Spaceman watch shown on page 193 was developed over the years. Its creator, André Le Marquand, modernized it by remodeling the case and strap to incorporate sharp corners. It was manufactured in Switzerland in 1974. The movement is mechanical and the watch is mounted directly onto the strap, a single piece of patent leather. The case is chromium-plated.

This mechanical watch is known as the stirrup watch and has Roman numerals, with the four indicated by IIII as is usual on clocks and watches. It is a Jaeger-LeCoultre made for Hermès, the elegant Paris fashion store, in the 1960s.

The Ventura by Hamilton is a little masterpiece of style that was marketed in various forms from 1957 through 1963. Inside the case, there is an electrical mechanism of the 500 series. The first watches in the Ventura series had two-tone straps (see page 315).

This Audemars Piguet Royal Oak self-winding watch has an octagonal bezel and crown. It was designed in the 1970s by Gérald Genta and is one of the great classics of the make. The strap is fitted with an expanding closure mechanism. The model also exists as a chronograph with a date aperture located between four and five o'clock (see page 130).

Ebel Président watch, with a very sophisticated design. The square dial is encased in red gold and the back is of steel. It was made in 1960.

Where watches are concerned, anything goes. Here are a few of the wackier styles, based on Disney and other cartoon characters. Of course, Mickey Mouse, symbol of eternal youth, started the ball rolling. This 1930 American-made Ingersoll watch was the first of its type. The mechanical movement drives hands that represent Mickey's arms. The strap is made of red vinyl.

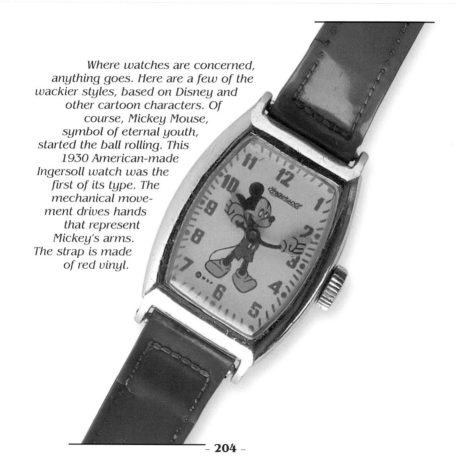

This model with a round dial is of more recent make than that on the facing page. These watches were often bottom-of-the-line models, but they served their purpose well enough.

Although long considered mere toys, these watches soon began to interest adults, who often enjoyed collecting them. The model on the left was produced in various versions in the 1960s, even as a fob watch (an example can be seen on page 31). The watches on the right were made in the 1970s and they differ mainly in the shape of the hands.

*These two watches have lost their straps,
but what fun it was for a child to learn to
tell the time with Donald Duck or Tintin.*

And here's Popeye the sailor man! This watch dates from 1965–1970 and is ideal for knowing when it's time for a snack, as long, of course, that it is spinach!

Very few of
these specialty
watches have
a rotating
bezel. This one
is made of
plastic and it is
just a gimmick. Mickey
and his pals are not the only
Disney characters to feature on
watches. Here we see Pinocchio.

To ensure you never missed any of those exciting episodes of Zorro, what better than this mechanical watch? Zorro's trusty steed serves as the center seconds hand. Of course, he moves around the dial like lightning!

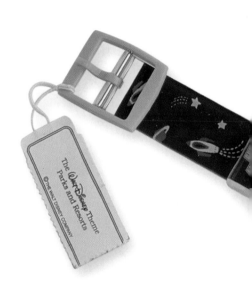

The Walt Disney Theme
Parks and Resorts
© THE WALT DISNEY COMPANY

These latter-day Disney watches feature the two heroes from the film Toy Story. They date from 1995 and both have a quartz digital movement. The face of Woody the sheriff lifts up to reveal the watch dial. The watch pictured below is luminous, evoking the futuristic world of Buzz, the space ranger. However, these watches are not exactly top-of-the range in terms of quality, and cannot be expected to last forever!

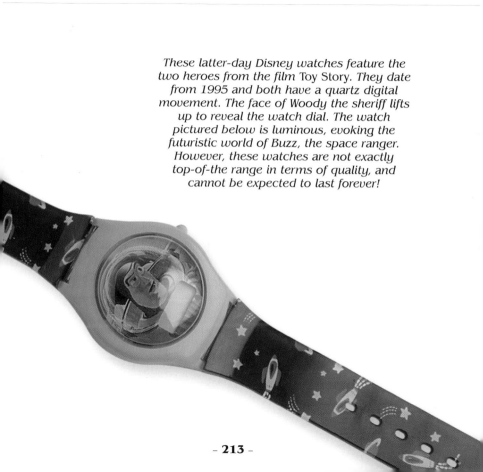

A Trot I
B Steeple
C Trot II

IV
PROFESSIONAL
watches

D ifferent people need different watches for different purposes. A deep-sea diver needs a very different type of watch from someone who simply dives into the bathtub, and a modern aviator flying at twice the speed of sound would find the good old "tick-tock" watches worn by First World War pilots to be sadly inadequate.

Many occupations thus require their own specialized watches. Those made for the military are among the most elaborate because they need to be particularly well suited to the harsh conditions of war and survival, whether at high altitude or in the ocean depths.

These special watches must be capable of withstanding unusual conditions, such as extremes of temperature. They must be shockproof, waterproof, and even impervious to the heat and sand of the desert.

This chronograph with two subsidiary dials is made by the Swiss firm of Heuer. During the 1970s, it was standard issue to German troops of the Bundeswehr attached to NATO. It has a flyback stopwatch feature. The black dial is marked "3-H," meaning that the luminous parts of the dial are painted with radium and are thus radioactive! The wrist-strap is the original one, and has a leather insert between the back of the case and the wrist.

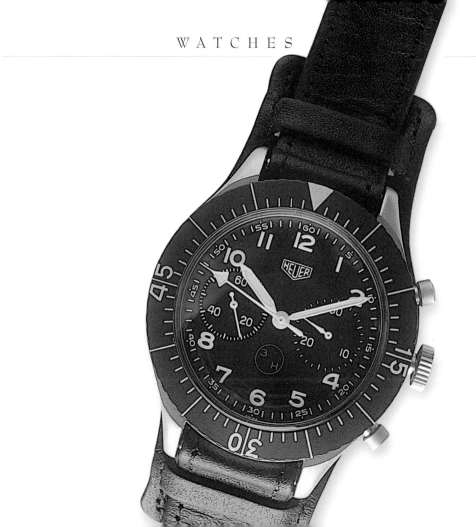

Another twin subsidiary dial chronograph by Heuer. The model was used by the Belgian Army serving in the Congo during the 1960s. This is the military version of the famous Carrera chronograph made by the firm. The dial is black and the Arabic numerals are luminous, so as to be easily read at night. The case is mounted on a leather strap and is made of steel with a screw-back case.

French military chronograph of the 1950s, made by J. Auricoste. It is a French watch assembled in Switzerland, a version of the famous Type 20 regulation watch. This one was made to a very rigorous specification produced by the French Ministry for the Armed Forces, for use by its troops. The mechanical movement is a Lemania. This model has a chromium-plated case. There is another, much rarer, version with a steel case.

An Avia watch made by the firm of Mimo in the 1930s. This early aviator's watch has a mechanical, anti-magnetic movement, and a subsidiary seconds dial at six o'clock. The metal case has a clip-on back. The dial is black and the numerals are Arabic.

Dodane chronograph, one of the Type 21 watches made for the French army. The name derives from the fact that this was the twenty-first specification for watches issued by the French government. There is a type 20 on page 219. The steel watch has a screw-back case on which the letters CEV are engraved, indicating that it was used by the French national flight-testing center. The Valjoux 222 mechanical movement provides the watch with a flyback function.

This Vixa type 20 watch was made in Germany in the 1950s. The case is steel, mounted on a leather strap. The Vixa watch was used by the French Air Force which imposed strict requirements on the suitability of the watch for use by navigators. The back of the case is therefore marked with a date and the letters FG, which stands for "fin de garantie" [end of warranty], at which time the watches had to be sent back to the manufacturer for overhaul. The Hanhart mechanical movement is antimagnetic and adapted to the extreme conditions of flight. The watch has a flyback function and a screw-back case.

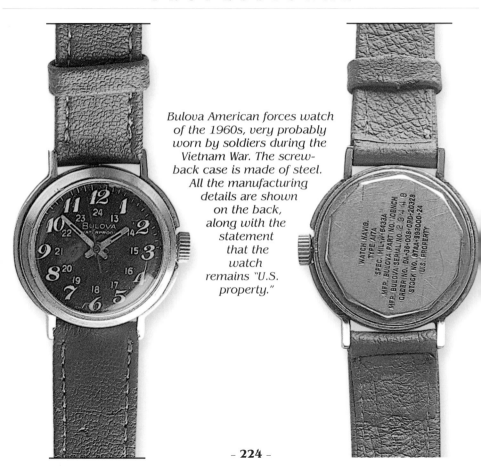

Bulova American forces watch of the 1960s, very probably worn by soldiers during the Vietnam War. The screw-back case is made of steel. All the manufacturing details are shown on the back, along with the statement that the watch remains "U.S. property."

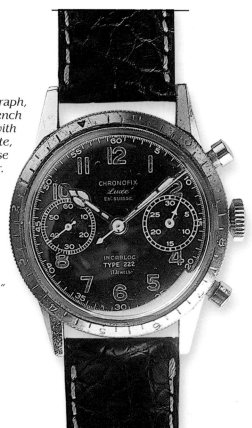

French army-issue chronograph, called a Chronofix. Since French troops were usually supplied with Dodane, Airain, Visa, Auricoste, and Breguet watches, these 1950s watches are much rarer. This Swiss-made Luxe model is a type 222 and has a black dial as well as two miniature dials and a flyback function. The bezel rotates on the steel case, and the watch is mounted on a leather strap. Note the rather unusual hands, described as "fly wings."

Watch made by the firm Lip, worn by French soldiers during World War I. This nickel-plated, Type Militaire watch is labeled on the enameled dial. The mechanical movement, of which the caliber is unknown, has an off-center subsidiary seconds hand dial at six o'clock. Note that, at the time, the fashion was for very narrow wrist-straps, unlike today's watches.

This is an American army watch of the same period that bears a striking resemblance to the French watch on the facing page. It is an Ingersoll with a base-metal case. The movement is mechanical and there is an off-center subsidiary seconds hand dial at six o'clock. Note the strongly protruding crown. The word "wrist" is inscribed on the dial to show that it is a wristwatch.

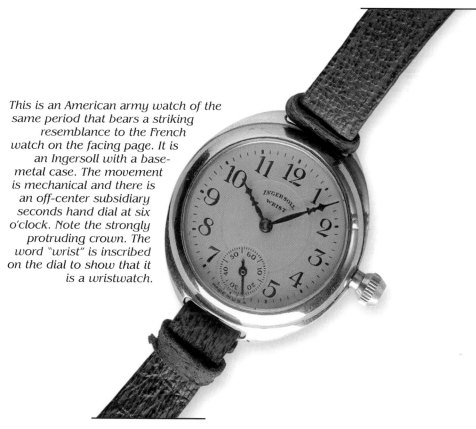

During World War I, early military wristwatches were manufactured with opening protective grilles over the dials. This watch dates from 1917, but the manufacturer is unknown. It is on display at the International Watch and Clock Museum at La Chaux-de-Fonds, Switzerland. The case is made of silver and bears the patent number 75066. The movement is Swiss.

The timepiece opposite is not exactly a wristwatch, because it was designed to be worn—on the knee! This precision instrument was to be worn by bomber pilots over their flying-suits. It is a Breitling chronograph made in the 1940s, with a heavy, rotating bezel and a dial divided into hectometers (10-meter sections) so that the pilot could measure the time it took for a projectile to fall to earth.

The Breitling Navitimer is a pilot's chrono-graph with a mechanical Vénus move-ment. It is supplied with various mea-suring scales, including a slide-rule to measure fuel and flying time. This model dates from the 1960s and the Breitling metal bracelet is the original one. This model is hard to find nowadays.

This 1952 Breitling Navitimer is a multifunctional precision instrument for air navigation. It was officially adopted by the Aircraft Owners and Pilots Association, and an almost identical model is still being made by this famous Swiss watchmaker.

A Russian chronograph with twin subsidiary dials dating from the 1970s, probably used by the Soviet air force. There is a date aperture at six o'clock. The main dial is pale gray. The watch has two crowns, one at three o'clock, to rewind the mechanical movement, the other at nine o'clock, to activate the revolving bezel located beneath the watch-glass. The inscription reads "Shturmanskie", meaning "Navigator's."

This Airain chronograph with twin subsidiary dials dates from the 1950s and was regulation issue for the French army. The inscription "Type 20" indicates that it complies with the relevant military specifications. It is a steel watch with a flyback function. The 17-ruby Valjoux 222 movement is mechanical and needs manual rewinding.

A chronograph with two push-buttons for the stopwatch function, made by the Swiss firm of Lemania. It was used by the Swedish army. There are twin subsidiary dials on the black dial. The case is made of steel with a notched rotating bezel that turns easily. This mechanical watch also has a Lemania movement.

Watch used by the French underwater explorer, Jacques Cousteau, for diving to depths of around 600 meters. It is an Omega Seamaster, made in 1970 and is also known to collectors as Ploprof. The one-piece case has a screw-in crown, which is located on the left so as not to impede the wrist movements of the diver. The numeral indicators and the dial are luminous, for easy reading at great depths. The rotating bezel is released by means of the red button on the right.

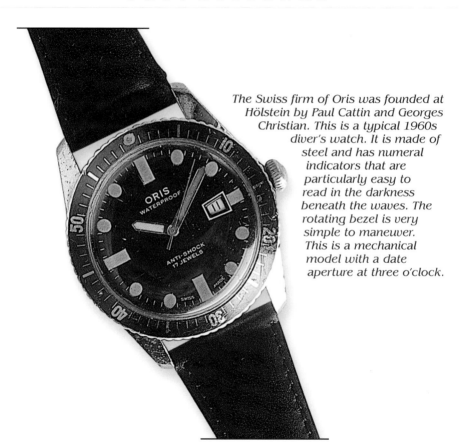

The Swiss firm of Oris was founded at Hölstein by Paul Cattin and Georges Christian. This is a typical 1960s diver's watch. It is made of steel and has numeral indicators that are particularly easy to read in the darkness beneath the waves. The rotating bezel is very simple to maneuver. This is a mechanical model with a date aperture at three o'clock.

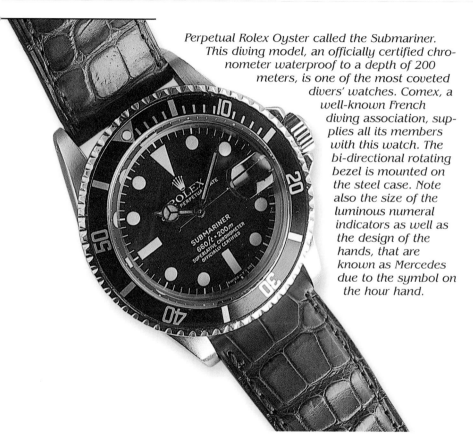

Perpetual Rolex Oyster called the Submariner. This diving model, an officially certified chronometer waterproof to a depth of 200 meters, is one of the most coveted divers' watches. Comex, a well-known French diving association, supplies all its members with this watch. The bi-directional rotating bezel is mounted on the steel case. Note also the size of the luminous numeral indicators as well as the design of the hands, that are known as Mercedes due to the symbol on the hour hand.

*Tudor steel diving watch with screw-in crown and
back. It is made by Rolex and is standard issue for
the French navy. This model was made in 1979 and
has a black dial. It bears a strong resemblance to ...*

... the Swiss-made Submariner model shown on page 237 and was also made with a blue dial. The black dial shown here is rarer.

This Bell & Ross Hydro Challenger 11,100 is made by the firm of Rosillo and Schmidt. It is of recent manufacture and its simple design is deceptive, in view of its technological prowess.

The watch is named for the Challenger Trench, an 11,100 meter-deep marine trench off the coast of Japan. The watch was capable of being taken down to that astonishing depth, thanks to the liquid silicone inside the case, which makes it uncompressible.

Here is another Omega diving chronograph. The automatic movement is mounted inside a particularly thick steel case. The watch was made in the 1970s and has the original chain-mail bracelet.

This Blancpain diver's watch was chosen by NATO in the 1970s for issue to German troops. It is made of steel and has an automatic movement and screw-back. The location of the crown, at four o'clock, is an unusual design feature. The watch is called Fifty Fathoms and is one of the best known models made by this Swiss firm.

Diver's watch made by Universal Genève, a Swiss firm founded in 1897 by Perret & Berthoud. It has a steel case with a screw-back and possesses the famous gold micro-rotor automatic movement. There are two crowns; the one located at two o'clock is for moving the rotating bezel beneath the watch-glass.

OW watch, water-proof at 1,000 meters. The monobloc steel case is of the Caribbean type. The bezel is very wide so that it can be rotated easily.

This Panerai Luminor GMT watch has a second set of numbers around the dial. The first of these watches was made in the 1930s and was fitted with a Rolex movement. It was used by naval divers in the Italian and German armies. Note the prominent crown locking system at three o'clock. The same watch, with an automatic movement and waterproof to 300 meters, is still being made today.

Raoul Dufy

VOUS QUI APPRECIEZ
LES VALEURS RÉELLES

vous choisirez une montre Longines, symbole de précision …
Vous aimez les lignes pures: le clacissisme de style du nouveau
«leader» Longines Flagship Automatic vous séduira d'emblée!

Le sens instinctif de la qualité – vertu prédominante chez les
horlogers de Longines – un esprit d'émulation entretenu de
génération en génération et une éthique: la vérité dans la
publicité comme en face de l'acheteur, ont permis d'assurer la
renommée et de maintenir dans le monde entier l'éminence
de la marque Longines.

Flagship Automatic concrétise aujourd'hui ce que seront les
exigences de demain.

V

AUTOMATIC

watches

For many, if not all, watch collectors, automatic watches represent the pinnacle of achievement in watchmaking technology. Automatic watches may also possess a whole range of other functions, such as being able to display the phases of the moon, dates, and even a perpetual calendar. All these features are well within the capabilities of an automatic watch, and in no way detract from its original function—measuring the passing of time. One other feature that has proved invaluable to many is complete waterproofing, which has saved from ruin the favorite watches of all sorts of people from deep-sea divers, fishermen and sailors, to homemakers at the kitchen sink!

The Rolls watch borrowed its name from the famous British luxury car, the Rolls Royce. In addition, the name hints at the fact that the rewinding movement is a "rolling" motion. This self-winding mechanism was invented by a Parisian named Léon Hatot and patented in 1930. The model shown here is of that same period and was manufactured by Blancpain in Switzerland. The crown is concealed beneath the wide bezel that can be raised when the watch needs to be adjusted.

This Glycine watch in its original chromium-plated case dates from the early 1930s. The hammer-shaped oscillating weight that automatically raises the barrel moves to and fro at 120°. The crown is located at three o'clock and is only used to adjust the hands that are of the so-called "fly-wing" type.

Steel 1960 Jaeger-LeCoultre watch. The aperture at twelve o'clock indicates the watch's power reserve, which in this case was a maximum of forty hours. The aperture turns red to warn the user when no more than fifteen hours are left.

Even a close inspection of this LeCoultre watch made in 1960 does not reveal the the whereabouts of a crown for adjusting the hands. In fact, the crown is hidden under the case. There is no need for a rewinding button, because the watch is self-winding and has a comfortable energy reserve of forty hours, indicated by the subsidiary dial at nine o'clock. The case is gold-filled.

The most important feature of this very handsome automatic LeCoultre is the power reserve aperture at twelve o'clock. The black dial shows alternate Arabic numerals and the case has a screw-back. The watch dates from the late 1950s and was aimed at the American market.

An automatic Jaeger-LeCoultre with gold case; the watch on the facing page is made of steel. This one has a banking movement and is of the same period. Both show the energy reserve at twelve o'clock.

This rare steel watch
dates from the late
1960s. It is a Jaeger-
LeCoultre divers'
watch made in France
and fitted with an ETA
movement made
by Jaeger.

These two Rolex Bubble Back watches were made in 1930–1935. The thick, luminous numerals on the dial are typical of the period, but the state-of-the-art automatic movement was one of the first to be patented. The screw-back cases are Oyster with screw-in crowns. Hands are the Mercedes style (see pages 237 and 238).

A Rolex Oyster Perpetual Datejust Turn-O-Graph manufactured in the late 1960s. The case is made of steel with the exception of the rotating bezel which is of gray-gold. This watch is also a certified chronometer.

The Rolex Sea-Dweller, big sister of the Submariner model, is waterproof to a depth of 1,220 meters below sea level. This performance has been verified, as recorded on the dial. This watch is of recent manufacture and is fitted with a gas escape valve and a sapphire crystal glass. This model is currently used by many professional deep-sea divers.

Although the name of Rolex is associated with luxury gold watches, there are several models that have steel cases. This is one of them, the Explorer I, made in 1967, reference number 1016. The original dial shows Roman numerals three, six, and nine. Note the matching steel Jubilee bracelet.

This Rolex Oyster Perpetual is an officially certified chronometer with a so-called honeycomb dial. It is made of eighteen-carat gold, with a screw-down crown and screw-back. This model dates from the 1950s. The various photographs of Rolex watches in this book show how the firm's logo has changed over the years.

It would be hard to find a more conservative or more reliable model than this all-steel Rolex Air King Precision. Note that there is not even a date-aperture under the sapphire crystal glass. Ever since the firm was founded by Hans Wilsdorf in Geneva in 1919, Rolex has made it a point of honor to sell only watches with the most accurate and reliable movements.

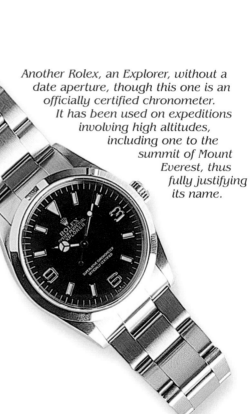

Another Rolex, an Explorer, without a date aperture, though this one is an officially certified chronometer. It has been used on expeditions involving high altitudes, including one to the summit of Mount Everest, thus fully justifying its name.

This Rolex wristwatch has an unusually shaped eighteen-carat yellow-gold case and a black dial. It is another Rolex model that has been officially recognized as being an automatic chronometer. The back of the case and the crown are screw-in. The watch was made in the 1950s.

This automatic Rolex Oyster Datejust has a Jubilee steel bracelet and was made in the 1980s. The bezel is milled and the dial is an unusual blue color.

Watches that display the time in an aperture, which were all the rage in the 1930s and 1940s, now look rather dated. Some people still favor this style. This automatic Tissot watch called the New Timer has an automatic rewinding mechanism. It dates from the late 1970s.

This Tissot Seastar, made around 1970, has such clean lines and harmonizes so well with its metal bracelet that it could have just as well been included in the section devoted to designer watches. It shows the day of the week and the date at three o'clock and has a central seconds hand. No numerals are shown on the dial.

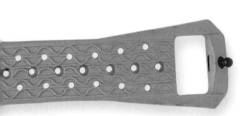

When this Tissot Sideral S first appeared on the market in 1975, it was considered avant-garde in style. The case is made of a composite and there is no removable back, the movement being inserted through the dial. Thanks to this original design, the watch is completely waterproof.

This Hamilton automatic chronograph has a movement similar to those used by Breitling and Heuer. There is nothing surprising in this because the movement was developed by Buren for all three firms.
The watch first went into production in 1969.

The first waterproof French watch is thought to have been made by Lip and used a case imported from Switzerland. It was a Nautic model, first manufactured in 1967. This version with an automatic movement is quite rare.

Automatic waterproof
watch dating from 1965.
It was manufactured
jointly by Lip and
Blancpain. The bezel
rotates and it has a
screw-back steel case.

This Omega Constellation is officially certified as a chronometer. It dates from the late 1960s. The very classic wristwatch style is much appreciated by collectors. The case is made of steel.

Another
Omega
Constellation
model that is
certified as
a chronometer. The
back of the case is
engraved with the attractive
design of an observatory whose
dome is surrounded by a constellation of
stars. The case is made of eighteen-carat
gold and has a faceted dial with a date-
aperture at three o'clock.

Omega Dynamic watch. The firm of Omega has been in existence for more than one hundred years. Several other models shown in this book demonstrate how the design of the case and dial were influenced by television. This is especially true of the clock that was shown on French television as a time check in the 1970s— the period during which this watch was made and sold. The date is shown at three o'clock. The dial is two-tone and the crown recessed.

The most important feature of a watch must be its readability. This Omega Seamaster is extremely easy to read, with its gilt numeral indicators, wedge-shaped hands, and large central seconds hand. Furthermore, it is has proved to be extremely accurate since it was first marketed in the mid-1950s.

This Zenith Port Royal has an automatic rewind feature, and displays the day and date. It is a very well-made watch, dating from the 1970s.

Automatic Zenith watch with a square case, marketed from 1960 through 1970. It displays the date and day of the week in French. The Zenith trademark was established in Switzerland in 1865 by Georges Favre-Jacquot, who recruited a staff of talented watchmakers.

The word "automatique" (automatic) is inscribed on the dial of this watch just above the trademark Zenith, followed by the number 28,800. This represents the frequency of the oscillation of the balance-wheel, a gauge of accuracy. This precision watch, displaying the date between four and five o'clock, thus claimed to have a very high-frequency movement.

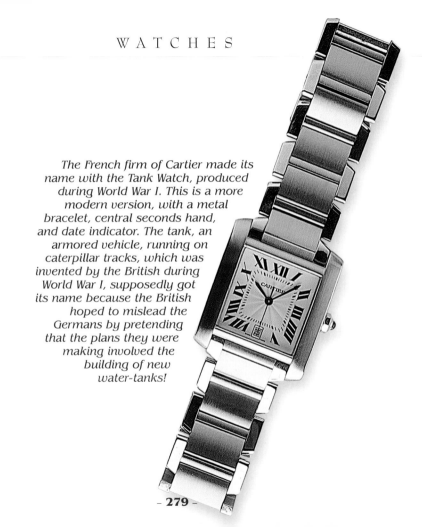

The French firm of Cartier made its name with the Tank Watch, produced during World War I. This is a more modern version, with a metal bracelet, central seconds hand, and date indicator. The tank, an armored vehicle, running on caterpillar tracks, which was invented by the British during World War I, supposedly got its name because the British hoped to mislead the Germans by pretending that the plans they were making involved the building of new water-tanks!

Several makes of automobile have given rise to watches bearing their name. The two industries have much in common, after all, with their emphasis on precision engineering. This chronograph with its three subsidiary dials and an aperture showing the date and day of the week was produced by Porsche Design, a firm owned by one of the sons of the founder of the Porsche automobile corporation. This automatic watch made by Orfina dates from 1978. It has a Lemania 5100 movement. The case is made entirely of black-anodized steel.

The French firm of Nicolet produced this
diving watch that is waterproof to a
depth of 300 meters and is fitted
with an automatic movement
inside a steel case. The black,
rotating bezel is the same
color as the dial. It dates
from the early 1970s.

Note the unobtrusive and discreet location of the date aperture replacing the numeral at three o'clock. When it is 3:00 A.M. or P.M. on the third day of the month, the display performs a dual function! This is a Universal Genève watch made in the 1950s.

On 24 February 1957, Scandinavian Airlines Systems (SAS) began operating its first service between Europe and the United States, flying over the North Pole. To mark the occasion, the crew members were presented with one of these 138-caliber automatic watches which, after the event, became known as the Polerouter model. It is a gold Swiss watch, a Universal Genève, fitted with a micro-rotor.

The automatic movement of this 1978 Movado watch operates at a high frequency (36,000 pulses per hour), twice the number of pulses of a regular watch of the period. It also shows the day of the week and the date at three o'clock. The model is named Video, due to the shape of the dial that resembles a television screen.

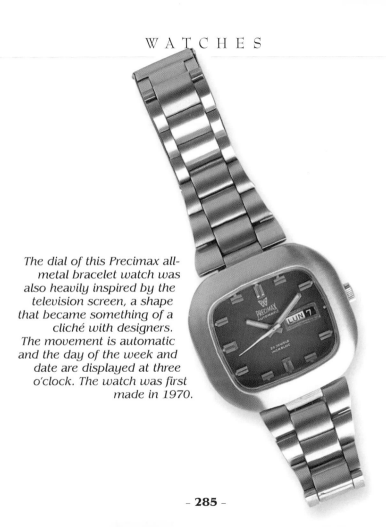

The dial of this Precimax all-metal bracelet watch was also heavily inspired by the television screen, a shape that became something of a cliché with designers. The movement is automatic and the day of the week and date are displayed at three o'clock. The watch was first made in 1970.

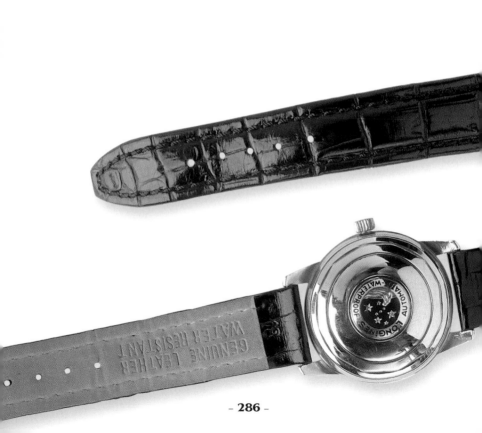

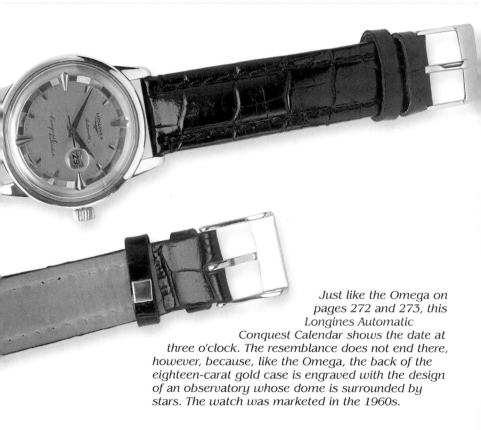

Just like the Omega on pages 272 and 273, this Longines Automatic Conquest Calendar shows the date at three o'clock. The resemblance does not end there, however, because, like the Omega, the back of the eighteen-carat gold case is engraved with the design of an observatory whose dome is surrounded by stars. The watch was marketed in the 1960s.

VI

ELECTRIC &
ELECTRONIC

watches

W atch- and clock-making very often preceded rather than followed the industrial technology of their time. So it is hardly surprising that in the age of nuclear energy, the industry searched for new sources of power. The crown, rewinding knob, and sophisticated automatic self-winding systems were discarded in favor of an electronically controlled movement that sounded the knell of the old "tick-tock" watch.

The American firm of Hamilton led the way as long ago as the 1950s when it produced the first electric watch. The tiny battery had enough power to enable the watch to run for a year. Then, in the 1970s, the quartz movement revolutionized the centuries-old watchmaking industry, almost destroying it overnight.

Note that the numeral indicators at each quarter hour on this dial are a clue to the nature of the movement. It is the product of two years of research, from 1957 through 1959, at the Ébauches company in Neuchâtel, Switzerland. This was the first electrically powered watch manufactured in Switzerland. The case is rolled gold with a screw-back.

*Longines Flagship
Ultronic, indicating
the days and date
at three o'clock. It
is a rolled gold
electronic watch
that was marketed
in the early 1970s.*

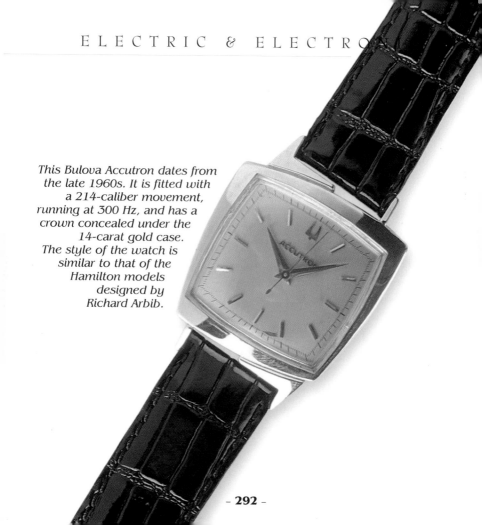

This Bulova Accutron dates from the late 1960s. It is fitted with a 214-caliber movement, running at 300 Hz, and has a crown concealed under the 14-carat gold case. The style of the watch is similar to that of the Hamilton models designed by Richard Arbib.

Rolled-gold
Bulova Accutron
dating from the late 1960s
and early 1970s. It was produced to
commemorate the hundredth
anniversary of the brand.

Another Bulova Accutron with a
214 movement that uses a
387 S battery. The case is
made of steel and the
fixed bezel is of gold.
The watch-glass is
silk-screen printed with
the numeral indicators,
obviating the need for
a dial and making it
possible to view the
mechanism inside this
Spaceview model.

This Bulova Accutron model
dates from 1969 and its
design is typical of these
very special watches.
It contains a Bulova
214 movement.
The case is rolled
gold but the back
is made of steel.

These three watches symbolize the inauguration of the era of electromagnetic watches. The electromagnetic compass system was designed to replace the balance-wheel on conventional watches. The system oscillates at a frequency of 300 Hz and through a quartz wheel, transforms the movement into a rotation (as in the model on the left on the facing page). The watch below is a quartz Bulova, as indicated by the name, Accuquartz. The electromechanical Miromax, on the far right, has a perpetual calendar. All these watches date from the 1970s.

Timex watch with
an electrical movement.
The crown is located on
the back of the case.
The dial shows the Roman
numerals 3, 6, 9, and 12 and
is plain enough to make the
time easy to read. This unused watch from the
1960s was sold in France and still bears its original
price tag in French francs.

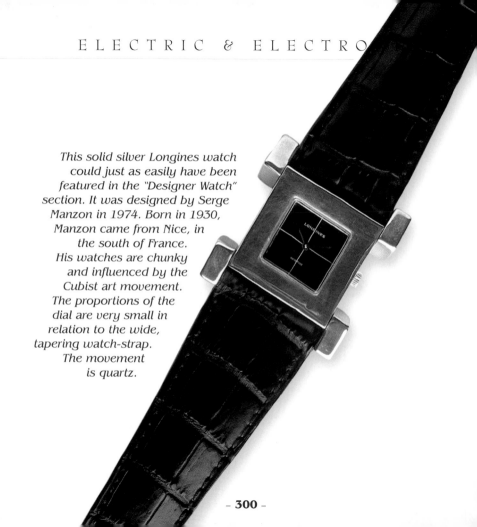

This solid silver Longines watch could just as easily have been featured in the "Designer Watch" section. It was designed by Serge Manzon in 1974. Born in 1930, Manzon came from Nice, in the south of France. His watches are chunky and influenced by the Cubist art movement. The proportions of the dial are very small in relation to the wide, tapering watch-strap. The movement is quartz.

swatch

MADE IN SWISS WATCH

Askan

12

9

6

swatch
SWISS

quartz
anche 3 atu
(30 m)
Antichoc

• Exactitud del
cuarzo
• Impermeable
3 atu (30 m)
• Resistente
a los choques

• Precisione
al quarzo
• Impermeabile
a 30 at

Although the Swatch is a recent invention, it soon became an institution. It is an inexpensive, amusing, plastic toy that represents the ideal medium for creativity. This 1988 model was designed by Valerio Adami for the Maeght Foundation for Contemporary Art that has its home in the town of Saint-Paul-de-Vence in the south of France. The movement is quartz.

Concepts of time and movement are behind the work of the Belgian artist, Pol Bury, so what could be more natural for him than to design a watch? This is a Swatch called Filtre. It dates from 1988.

Many artists and designers from a variety of backgrounds have produced designs for Swatch. The dial of this model has been decorated by the French artist Pierre Alechinsky. His fascination with the arts of calligraphy and typography are clearly in evidence here.

The Chrono Flash Arrow that Swatch first marketed in 1990 was an immediate hit. It differed little esthetically from classic models, but its quartz ETA movement made it an accurate chronograph. This model, shown here in the original presentation box, was one of the first to be manufactured.

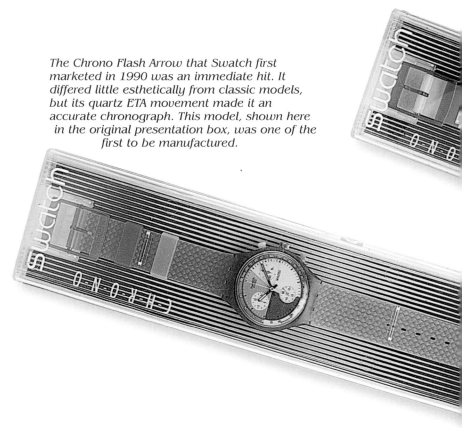

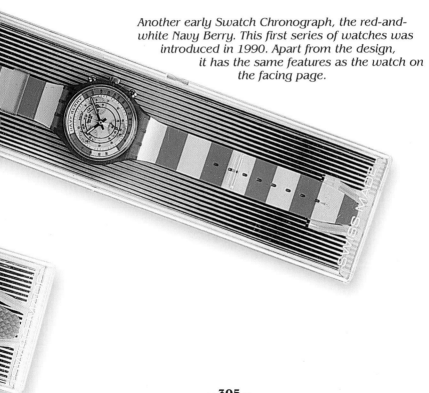

Another early Swatch Chronograph, the red-and-white Navy Berry. This first series of watches was introduced in 1990. Apart from the design, it has the same features as the watch on the facing page.

*This is another
Swatch, a fantasy
Pop model this
time, again in the
original box. Launched
in 1986, it is inspired
by aviator watches.
One innovation is the elastic
strap that is removable so the
watch can be worn as a fob. In
addition to the flamboyant colors,
note the crown at twelve o'clock.*

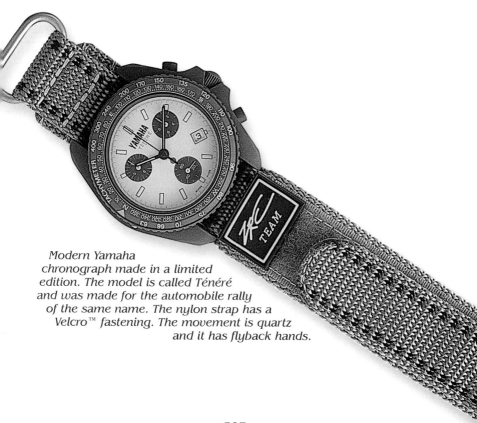

Modern Yamaha
chronograph made in a limited
edition. The model is called Ténéré
and was made for the automobile rally
of the same name. The nylon strap has a
Velcro™ fastening. The movement is quartz
and it has flyback hands.

*This electric, 32-Khz
Omega Constellation watch
dates from the early 1980s.
The case is made of steel and is
mounted on a leather strap. It has an
aperture showing the day and date.*

*Like many other famous
watchmakers, Omega has attempted originality in its
models. This Equinoxe model dates from the early 1980s and
has a dual face. On one side it shows the classic dial with
hands, and on the other a digital display. The faces are changed
by sliding the case dial across the case.*

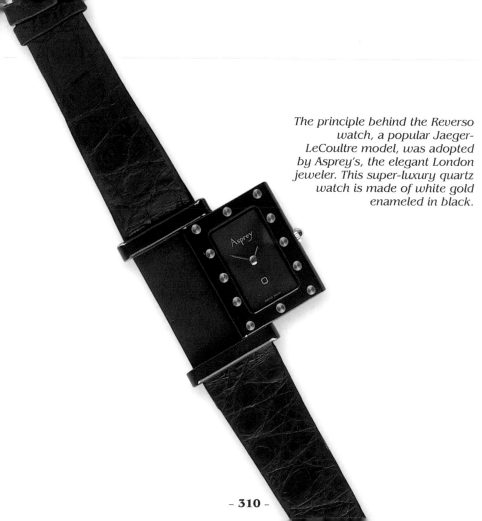

The principle behind the Reverso watch, a popular Jaeger-LeCoultre model, was adopted by Asprey's, the elegant London jeweler. This super-luxury quartz watch is made of white gold enameled in black.

It dates from the 1980s and only ten copies were made. The hidden side of the dial has a domino design on it, in which the number of dots indicates the number of this limited edition.

The most prestigious firms of watchmakers such as Universal Genève were overwhelmed by the new fashion for electronic watches. This model uses the tuning-fork electromechanical system.

This is a Zenith tuning-fork electromechanical movement, an XL-Tronic model that uses the Swiss-designed movement patented by Bulova. The television-screen shape of the dial is typical of the period, placing it firmly in the late 1970s. There is a date and day of the week aperture at three o'clock.

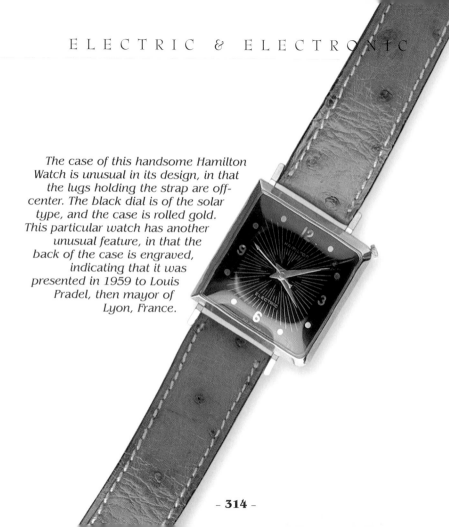

The case of this handsome Hamilton Watch is unusual in its design, in that the lugs holding the strap are off-center. The black dial is of the solar type, and the case is rolled gold. This particular watch has another unusual feature, in that the back of the case is engraved, indicating that it was presented in 1959 to Louis Pradel, then mayor of Lyon, France.

Like the watch on the facing page, this is a Richard Arbib design. It is a rolled-gold Hamilton, an American make, produced in 1957. The leather strap is gilded on the left half, black on the right, to echo the black dial with its gold numeral indicators. When first made, it was dubbed "the watch of the future," since it was the first electric watch to be produced industrially. Note the symbol linking three o'clock and nine o'clock, representing electric resistance.

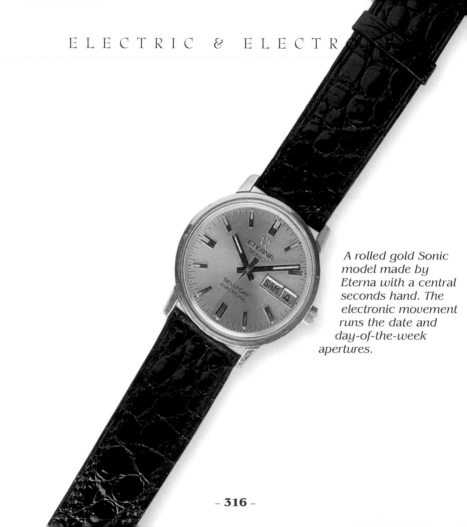

A rolled gold Sonic
model made by
Eterna with a central
seconds hand. The
electronic movement
runs the date and
day-of-the-week
apertures.

This 1963 model was the first battery-operated electro-mechanical watch made by Lip. The Lip watches, which had an R148 movement, featured a lightning flash on the dial to indicate the type of movement. In 1959, the brand advertising claimed "Lip electronic needs no rewinding ... ever."

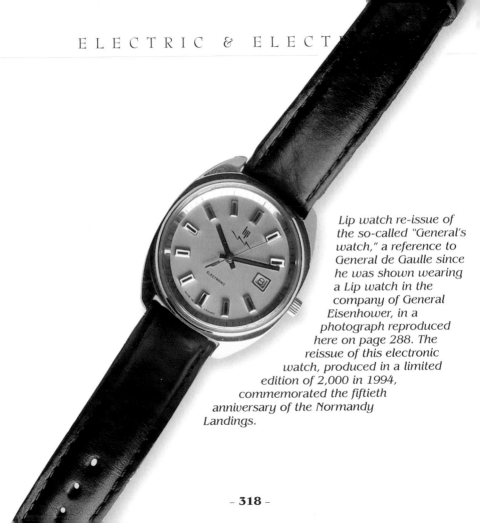

Lip watch re-issue of the so-called "General's watch," a reference to General de Gaulle since he was shown wearing a Lip watch in the company of General Eisenhower, in a photograph reproduced here on page 288. The reissue of this electronic watch, produced in a limited edition of 2,000 in 1994, commemorated the fiftieth anniversary of the Normandy Landings.

Replacement vehicles lent by dealers and garages to motorists whose automobiles are being repaired are a well-known practice. However, in 1963–1964, the French watchmakers, Lip, had a watch that served the same purpose. The Après-Vente (After-Sales) model was fitted with an R148 electromechanical movement.

This great classic of
the 1960s is a steel
case Lip Nautic-Ski with
a screw-back. It is a
diver's watch with an interior
bezel that can be rotated by means of
the crown located at two o'clock.
The movement is a Lip R 184.

Collectors should not forget the importance of commemorative watches or those presented at inaugurations. This one was a free gift to journalists to mark the opening of the Motoring Museum at Mougins, near Cannes, on the French Riviera.

From the 1970s onward, "giftwatches" became popular. Before this date, accurate timepieces were too expensive to be dispensed to all and sundry. As soon as it became possible to manufacture watches cheaply, every firm, every organization, and even government departments had the idea of presenting them to all comers. This rather unusual example was given out by the French Ministry of the Interior.

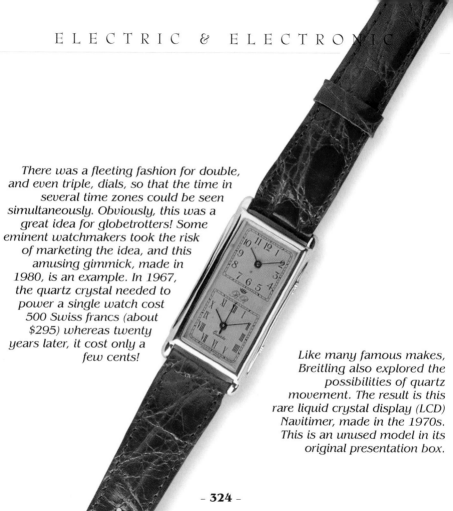

There was a fleeting fashion for double, and even triple, dials, so that the time in several time zones could be seen simultaneously. Obviously, this was a great idea for globetrotters! Some eminent watchmakers took the risk of marketing the idea, and this amusing gimmick, made in 1980, is an example. In 1967, the quartz crystal needed to power a single watch cost 500 Swiss francs (about $295) whereas twenty years later, it cost only a few cents!

Like many famous makes, Breitling also explored the possibilities of quartz movement. The result is this rare liquid crystal display (LCD) Navitimer, made in the 1970s. This is an unused model in its original presentation box.

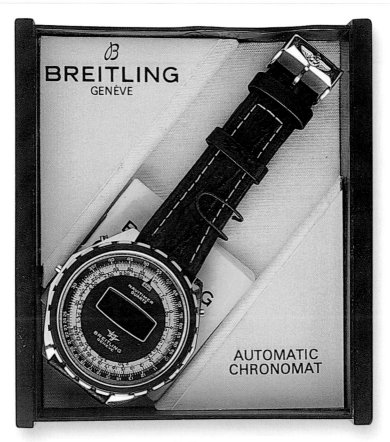

This watch must have been specially made for hairdressers! At any rate, the model, produced in 1990, has hands in the shape of a pair of scissors.

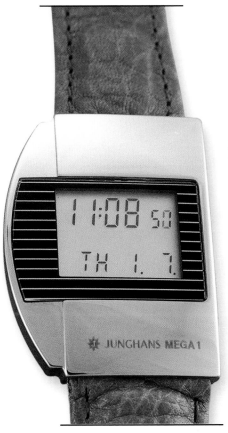

This 1990 watch by Junghans is radio-controlled. The quartz movement is fitted with a miniature receiver that during the night (at exactly 2:00 A.M.) detects time signals emitted from Frankfurt, thanks to an antenna hidden in the strap. It is thus maintained constantly at exactly the right time. The liquid crystal display indicates not only the time but also the day of the week, the date, the month, and the time in a second time zone.

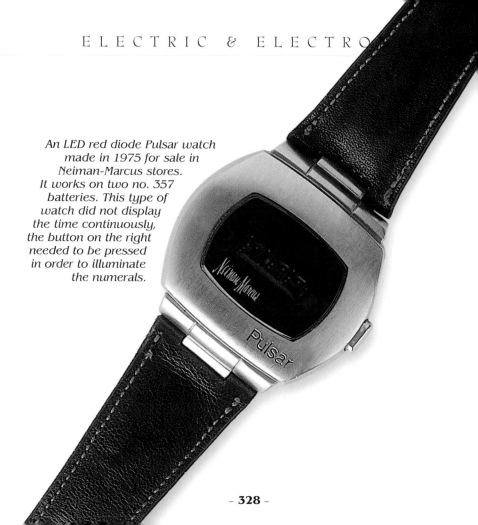

An LED red diode Pulsar watch made in 1975 for sale in Neiman-Marcus stores. It works on two no. 357 batteries. This type of watch did not display the time continuously, the button on the right needed to be pressed in order to illuminate the numerals.

A 1974 Omega red diode watch.
The case and bracelet are made of
steel and it has two push-buttons.
The right-hand button shows the
time, the one on the left displays
the date and month.
The movement was
made by Bulova and
adapted by Omega.

This Sicura is totally ecological, because it operates on power from the sun's rays! The case and bracelet are made of steel. The solar panel is built into the case on the right-hand side. There is also a day of the week and date aperture.

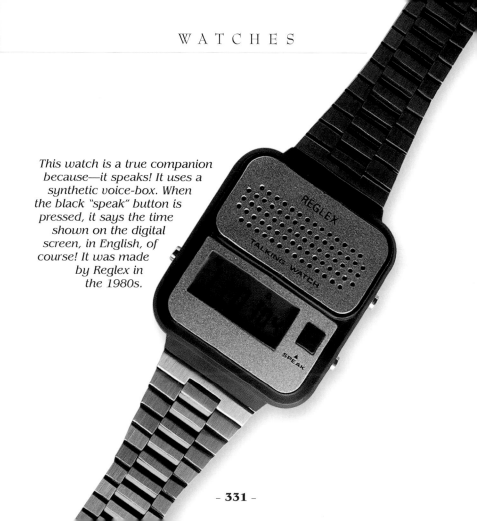

This watch is a true companion because—it speaks! It uses a synthetic voice-box. When the black "speak" button is pressed, it says the time shown on the digital screen, in English, of course! It was made by Reglex in the 1980s.

This Calculator watch was made by Pulsar in 1977. Shown here in its original presentation case, the watch came with a special pen-stylus for pressing the miniaturized buttons below the dial. Unfortunately, it was very power-hungry, requiring four 357-type batteries for operation.

In the modernist trend of the 1970s, every kind of trick was used to tempt the purchaser who could then amaze his friends by showing them the ingenious features of his new toy. At the time, red diode display, such as the one in this Jaz watch, was a real novelty. The display is activated by the top button on the right.

VII

COMPLEX

watches

There has always been huge competition among watchmakers who vie with each other, adding ever more complex features to their creations in the hope of astonishing and attracting new customers by their ingenuity. One of the first such features was an alarm system, introduced as long ago as the seventeenth century. Shortly thereafter came the perpetual calendar, another ingenious innovation. Such a watch is "programmed" to provide accurate information until well into the third millennium! Other functions and features followed. These include automatic alarms, flyback hands, catch-up chronographs, and miniature subsidiary dials to measure other timed events. All these mechanisms had to fit into the same, tiny space—a true feat of engineering!

Picard-Cadet is a Swiss make that ceased manufacture in the late 1980s. The watch that bears its logo has a Valjoux 7751 movement, a chronograph that indicates the date, and other complex features. A complex watch with a carefully planned design.

This complex Marc Nicolet chronograph was first sold in the 1970s. The day, month, and date are displayed, as are the phases of the moon. The case is made of steel. The main dial is gray and uses Arabic numerals.

This Omega automatic watch was only ever manufactured in a very limited edition. It is inscribed with the name of Louis Brandt, who founded the firm in 1848. This 1980 version is in eighteen-carat solid gold. It is extremely complex, with subsidiary dials for a perpetual calendar, the day of the week, the month, and the phases of the moon. Of course, it takes account of leap years.

The firm that
adopted the
name of Universal
Genève was called
Perret & Berthoud
until the late
nineteenth century.
This watch, made
around 1940, has an
annual calendar and
possesses a number of
other timed features such
as the phases of the moon.
It is made of eighteen-carat gold.

*Audemars Piguet produced a large number of
models in the Royal Oak range. This one is an
automatic watch that indicates the day, the
month, the date, and the phase of the moon.
The screwed-on bezel and the octagonal shape
make it a very masculine watch.*

This Léon Rochet automatic chronograph displays all the time-related events, the month, day of the week, date, and phase of the moon. The movement used in this model is a Valjoux 7750. The watch is currently still available in the stores.

A 1940s Jaeger-LeCoultre watch made of eighteen-carat red gold. The apertures display the day of the week (Thursday in this case) and the month (June). The red-and-white needle points to an inner dial indicating the date (27 in this case). All that is missing is the year. The mechanical watch has a seconds off-center subsidiary dial at six o'clock.

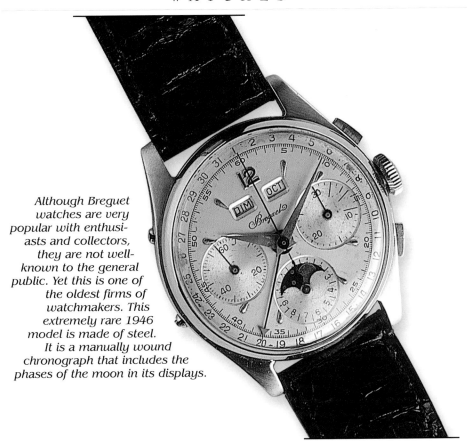

Although Breguet watches are very popular with enthusiasts and collectors, they are not well-known to the general public. Yet this is one of the oldest firms of watchmakers. This extremely rare 1946 model is made of steel. It is a manually wound chronograph that includes the phases of the moon in its displays.

Tricompax stop-watch by Universal Genève, a complex watch in eighteen-carat red gold, with a mechanical winding mechanism. It displays the day, month, and date, as well as the phases of the moon. This chronograph was manufactured between 1945 and 1950.

This fairly recent, simplified design is by Jaeger-LeCoultre and has a power reserve aperture at twelve o'clock. Such an indicator can be classified as a complex feature. This is an eighteen-carat gold watch dating from the 1960s.

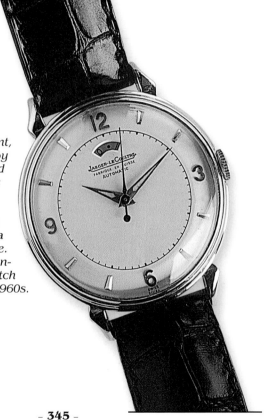

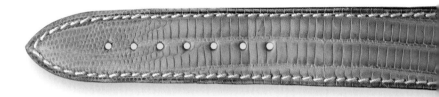

This triple-indicator watch shows the day of the week, the month, and the date. There is another complexity, however. The subsidiary dial at six o'clock shows the time in a second time zone. This recently manufactured automatic Swiss watch is unmarked. Only the strap is shown to have been made in Paris. A sapphire crystal aperture in the back of the watch make it possible to admire its sophisticated mechanism.

*The smaller the space and
volume with which the
watchmaker has to work, the
more amazing the feats he
performs. This Audemars
Piguet watch displays a
perpetual day of the week,
month, and phase of the
moon with leap years
programmed in until...*

...2100! The square dial is set in an eighteen-carat gold case. The watch was only produced in limited numbers and has a mechanical rewind. As with the watch on the previous page, the transparent back makes it possible to admire the intricate miniaturized mechanism.

The back of this gold watch is glass, so that the no. 85 gilt movement with manual rewind can be viewed. This Blancpain watch has a complex repeater system that chimes faintly on the hour, half-hour, and minutes. It was made in Switzerland in 1996.

This Movado Calendomatic has a Factories C 225 movement and also shows the day of the week and date (in this case, in Italian). It was manufactured in La-Chaux-de-Fonds, Switzerland, in around 1950. The three concentric circles of the figures on the dial indicate, starting from the center, the hours, minutes, seconds, and the date. There are apertures for the day of the week and the months.

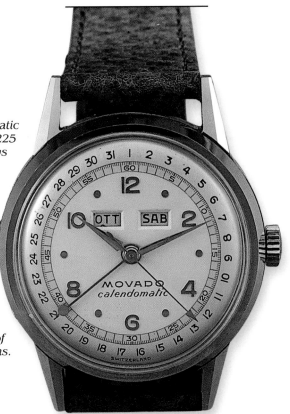

This handsome timepiece, displayed in the International Watch- and Clockmaking Museum of La-Chaux-de-Fonds, is a Vacherin Constantin, made in 1992. The movement is known as skeletal. It has many complex features. The exposed dial consists of four painted metal circles that feature the months at the top, the dates on the right, and the phases of the moon at the bottom. The left-hand dial shows the days of the week, in English. It is self-winding.

Revue Thommen alarm watch made in 1997. The case is platinum and is waterproof to a depth of 30 meters. The dial is of silvered metal, with engine-turned decoration in the center. It bears the name Cricket and the number 047. The inner circle indicates the time at which the alarm will ring.

This Blancpain watch dates from 1993. It has a tourbillon mechanism that can be seen on the dial. This is an ingenious movement invented by Abraham-Louis Breguet in 1801, making it possible to compensate for operating errors that might arise due to constant changes in the position of the watch. The self-winding mechanism can store energy for up to eight days.

This watch has a special alarm system. The wavy hand points to the alarm time, inside the first concentric circle, that is set by turning the lower crown. The Oris brand specialized in watches in the mid-price range.

This gold wristwatch was made by Girard-Perregaux. It has a tourbillon movement with a recessed, engraved bezel. The three gold strips across the face each have a central ruby. This ingenious system of bars, created by Constant Girard-Perregaux in the 1860s, holds the barillet, center wheel, and tourbillon cage in place.

Another complex Girard-Perregaux watch, known as a perpetual equation watch. The case is gold and the light-colored dial is divided into two, the outer part showing the twelve months of the year, the corresponding seasons, the solstices, and the equinoxes. The subsidiary dial located between ten o'clock and two o'clock is a perpetual calendar indicating the length of the month and the phase of the moon. The watch has a glass back so that the movement can be admired.

This is an automatic watch made by Kelek. The gadrooned gold case has six knobs for adjusting the time for the perpetual calendar and two more for the stopwatch function. The subsidiary dial at twelve o'clock shows the seconds, the date, and the seasons, and the subsidiary dial at six o'clock shows the day of the week (in French) and the hour. The third subsidiary dial, located at nine o'clock, shows the months and leap years, and it is also a minute-counter. The fourth subsidiary dial, located at three o'clock, shows the phases of the moon and the number of the week in the current year.

This Polyplan model made by Movado also counts as a complex watch because the movement has had to be adapted to fit the strange shape of the case and the curved back. This is a manually wound watch on which even the crown is in an unusual position, inside the bottom lug. The lugs are made of silver wire and are soldered to the case.

Polished gold watch made by the International Watch Company (IWC). The automatic movement includes a perpetual calendar programmed to the year 2100. This watch is also a two-button stopwatch displaying the day of the week, the date, the week and the month, as well as the phase of the moon. The gear-wheels responsible for the moon phases are particularly accurate, losing or gaining a day only once every twenty-two years. An aperture at seven o'clock displays the year.

The steel-case Nivada Grenchen watch shown here has an alarm function. The hand tipped with an arrow that points to six o'clock shows the time set for the alarm. The watch is waterproof and mounted on a leather strap. The bezel rotates.

Alarm watches are always classified as complex watches. This Vulcain, a Cricket model, is a good example. It was made in the 1960s and is fitted with a Vulcain movement. A watch of this type was presented to each president of the United States at the beginning of his term of office. Few appear to have worn them, however.

This Jaeger-LeCoultre Memovox has an alarm and an automatic movement. The watch was made around 1965 and has two crowns, one of which is used to operate the central disk on which a triangular arrow indicates the time at which the alarm will sound.

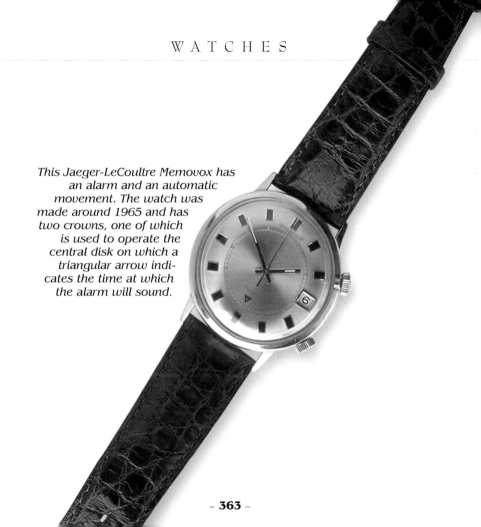

Two Jaeger-LeCoultre watches, both Memovox models. The one on the facing page was made in the 1960s and has a steel screw-back case. The movement is automatic. The one on this page was made in the 1940s and the case is eighteen-carat gold. It has a mechanical movement with manual rewind and a central seconds hand.

*Both watches use an
alarm system operated
by using an additional
crown to adjust a disk in
the center of the watch.
The Memovox alarm
watch was one of the
best-selling lines
produced by the Swiss
manufacturer during
the 1960s.*

Jaeger-LeCoultre Memovox model made in the 1950s. The steel-case watch has a mechanical movement. The central seconds hand is attached to the central disk on which the alarm indicator is marked.

It is rare for a watch possessing an alarm to be sufficiently waterproof for classification as a diver's watch. This steel-case Tissot with a clip-on back is a good example of such a watch.

Cricket,
an alarm watch
with a mechanical
movement, was made by
Revue-Thommen, a firm later
acquired by Vulcain. The model
first appeared in 1947 and is
traditionally presented to the
presidents of the United States when
they take office (see page 362).

The movement in this Royce watch, made in 1976, is fairly complex. This Twin-Matic model has an alarm as well as a display for the date and day.

Index, Addresses & Bibliography

Watch collector Marie-Pia Coustans and a selection of her watches from the French firm of Lip.

Index

The index includes the principal makes and models featured in this book.

Accuquartz (Bulova), 296
Accutron (Bulova), 24,
    292–293, 294–295
Air King (Rolex), 260
Airain, 233
Après-Vente (Lip), 319
Audemars Piguet, 43, 130,
    202, 340, 348–349
Auricoste (J.), 219
Autavia (Heuer), 115
Automatic Conquest Calendar
    (Longines), 287
Avia (Mimo), 220

Bell & Ross, 124–125, 240
Blancpain, 20, 156, 242, 270,
    350, 354
Breguet, 20, 47, 120–121,
    343
Breitling, 20, 22, 68,
102–103, 104–105, 106,
108–109, 110, 230–231, 325

Bubble Back (Rolex), 255
Buckingham (Corum), 197
Bulova, 24, 75, 138, 224,
    292–293, 294–295, 296

Cadette (Breitling), 108
Calatrava (Patek
    Philippe), 97
Calculator (Pulsar), 332
Candides (Lip), 175
Carrera (Heuer), 118, 154,
    218
Cartier, 20, 70–71, 72–73, 94,
    134, 279
Challenger 11 100 (Bell &
    Ross), 240
Chrono Flash Arrow
    (Swatch), 304
Chronofix, 225
Chrono-Matic (Breitling),
    104–105
Citizen, 192

Colani, 196
Constellation (Omega), 271,
    272–273, 308
Copilote (Breitling), 103
Corum, 21, 36, 197
Cosmique (Lip), 182
Cosmonaute (Breitling),
    106
Cricket (Revue Thommen),
    353, 368
Cricket (Vulcain), 362
Cyma, 85

Dauphine (Lip), 88–89
Daytona (Rolex), 148
Derby (Jaz), 169
Disney, 204–5, 206–207,
    208, 210–211, 212–213
Dodane, 221
Drivers (Pierre Cardin),
    188–189
Dynamic (Omega), 274

INDEX

Ébauches, 302
Ebel, 20, 40–42, 203
Eberhard, 131
Edox, 161
El Primero (Zenith), 155
Elves, 45, 99
Enicar, 157
Équinoxe (Omega), 309
Eterna, 18, 316
Étrier (Jaeger-LeCoultre, Hermès), 200
Explorer (Rolex), 261
Explorer I (Rolex), 258

Famoso, 163
Favre-Leuba, 146
Fifty Fathoms (Blancpain), 242
Filtre (Swatch), 302
Flagship Ultronic (Longines), 291
Flipper (Fortis), 21
Flyback (Blancpain), 156
Fortis, 21
Fresard, 162

Girard-Perregaux, 356–357

Glycine, 249
Gu(h)rke (Pop Swatch, Alfred Hofkunst), 194

Hamilton, 20, 24, 201, 268, 314–315
Hermès, 200
Heuer, 115, 116–117, 118–119, 154, 226–227, 218

Ingersoll, 204, 227
International Watch Company (IWC), 360
IroneK, 44

J.P. WalthierCo Elgin, 57
Jaeger, 49, 111, 113, 114
Jaeger-LeCoultre, 18, 20, 36, 46, 48, 50–51, 52–53, 54–55, 56, 69, 76, 112, 200, 250–251, 252–253, 254, 310–311, 342, 345, 363, 364–365, 366
Jaz, 169, 171, 333
Julien Gallet Co., 37
Junghans, 327

Kelek, 358
Képi (Lip), 87

Lemania, 150, 234
Léon Rochet, 341
Lip, 78, 81, 82–83, 84, 86–87, 88–89, 90–91, 93, 164–165, 168, 174–175, 176–177, 178–179, 180–181, 182–183, 184–185, 186–187, 226, 269, 270, 317, 320–321, 332–333
Longines, 20, 79, 136, 287, 291, 300
Louis Brandt (Omega), 338
Luminor GMT (Panerai), 245

Mach 2000 (Lip), 178–179
Marc Nicolet, 281, 337
Memovox (Jaeger-LeCoultre), 18, 363, 364–365, 366
Mickey Mouse, 204–205, 206–207
Mimo, 220
Miromax, 132, 296
Monaco (Heuer), 116–117
Moonwatch (Omega), 145

INDEX

Movado, 64, 284, 351, 359

Nautic (Lip), 269
Nautic-Ski (Lip), 320–321
Navitimer (Breitling), 230–231, 325
Navy Berry (Swatch), 305
New-Timer (Tissot), 264
Nivada Grenchen, 361

O.W., 244
Off-shore (Audemars Piguet), 130
Omega, 20–21, 62–63, 128–129, 140–141, 142–143, 145, 151, 245, 241, 271, 272–273, 274–275, 287, 308–309, 329, 338
Orfina, 122, 280
Oris, 20, 236, 355
Oyster (Rolex), 58–59, 247, 256, 259, 263

Pacha (Cartier), 134
Panerai, 245
Patek Philippe, 20–21, 28, 92–93, 95, 96–97

Péquignet (Émile), 67
Peugeot (Paul), 74
Picard-Cadet, 336
Pierce, 107
Pierre Cardin, 188–189
Polerouter (Universal Genève), 283
Poljot, 242
Polyplan (Movado), 359
Pop (Swatch), 306
Pop Swatch (Alfred Hofkunst), 194
Popeye, 209
Porsche Design, 122–123, 280
Port-Royal (Zenith), 276
Precimax, 139, 285
Premier (Breitling), 102
President (Ebel), 203
Pulsar, 328, 332

Ralco, 172
Record Watch, 77
Reglex, 331
Research Idea 2001 (Tissot), 190
Reverso (Jaeger-LeCoultre), 29, 46, 49, 310–311

INDEX

Revue-Thommen, 353, 368
Rolex, 58–59, 60–61, 156, 198, 237, 255, 256–257, 258–259, 260–261, 262–263
Rolls, 248
Royal Oak (Audemars Piguet), 202, 340
Royce, 369

S.D.H., 137
Saisons (Lip), 174
Sam, 78
Schild Frères, 37
Sea-Dweller (Rolex), 257
Seamaster (Omega), 143, 235, 275
Seastar (Tissot), 147, 265
Seiko, 20, 133
Sicura, 166–167, 330
Sideral S (Tissot), 267
Skipper (model Lip), 186
Sonic (Eterna), 316
Spaceman (Tressa Lux), 193, 199
Speedmaster (Omega), 129, 142, 145, 151
Square (Cartier), 73
Submariner (Rolex), 237, 238, 257

Swatch, 21, 27, 301, 302–303, 304–305, 306

Taboo-Taboo, 326
Tank (Cartier), 279
Tavannes, 85
Télévision (Lip), 183
Ténéré (Yamaha), 307
Timex, 298–299
Tintin, 208
Tissot, 20, 147, 190–191, 264–265, 266–267, 367
Top Time (Breitling), 109
Tortue (Cartier), 71
Tressa Lux, 193
Tricompax (Universal Genève), 344
Tudor, 238–239
Turn-O-Graph (Rolex), 256
Twin-Matic (Royce), 369
Type Militaire (Lip), 226
Type XX (Breguet), 120

Ulysse Nardin, 149
Universal Genève, 243, 282–283, 312, 339, 344

Vacheron Constantin, 20, 32, 66, 352

Vendôme (Cartier), 72
Ventura (Hamilton), 201
Verdu(h)ra, (Pop Swatch, Alfred Hofkunst), 194
Vidéo (Movado), 284
Vixa, 222–223
Vulcain, 362, 368

Waltham, 195
Wing Commander (Colani), 196

XL-Tronic, 313

Yachtingraf (Yema), 126
Yamaha, 307
Yema, 126–127, 160

Zenith, 20, 98, 152–153, 154–155, 276–277, 278, 313

Addresses

The following is a list of addresses that will help you find out more about your favorite subject.

MUSEUMS AND ASSOCIATIONS

American Clock and Watch Museum
100, Maple St.
Bristol, CT 06010
USA
Tel.: (203) 583-6070

American Watchmaker's and
Clockmaker's Institute
701, Enterprise Drive
Harrison, OH 45030-1696
USA
Tel.: (513) 367-9800

National Watch and Clock Museum
514, Poplar St.
Columbia, PA 17512-2130
USA
Tel.: (717) 684-8261
Also home to the National Association
of Watch and Clock Collectors.
www.nawcc.org

British Horological Institute
Upton Hall
Upton, Newark
Notts NG23 5TE
UK
Tel.: 01636 813 795

Prescot Museum of Clock and
Watchmaking
34 Church St
Prescot, Merseyside L34 3LA
UK
Tel.: 0151 430 7787

British Watch and Clock Collector's
Association
5, Cathedral Lane
Truro, Cornwall TR1 2QS
UK
Tel.: 01872 264 010

International Watch and Clock Museum
Rue des Musées 29,
2301 La Chaux-de-Fonds, Switzerland
Tel.: 032 967 68 61

SPECIALIST DEALERS

Air Clocks and Watches of the World
115, W 17th St
New York, NY 10011
Tel.: (212) 206-0077
USA

Cool Vintage Watches
5510 NE Antioch Rd

Cool Vintage Watches
5510 NE Antioch Road
Kansas City, MO 64119, USA
Tel.: (877) 856 1173

Harper's Jewellers
2/6, Minister Gates
York YO1 2HL, UK
Tel.: 01904 632 634

Miles Pocket Watches
PO Box 2608
Leesburg, VA 20177, USA
Tel.: (540) 338 5482

Royal Arcade Watches
4, Royal Arcade
London W1S 4SD, UK
Tel.: 0207 495 4882

SELECTED INTERNET SITES

www.horology.com
www.clockswatches.com
www.watchzone.net
www.watchnet.com

www.clockmakers.org
www.chronometer.net
www.watchblvd.com

AUCTION HOUSES
Certain auction houses hold special sales on a regular basis, where you can bid for rare and antique wristwatches:

Bonham's
Montpelier Street
Knightsbridge
London SW7 1HH, UK
Tel.: 0207 393 3900

Christie's
85, Old Brompton Road
London SW7 3LD, UK
Tel.: 0207 581 7611

Christie's USA
20, Rockefeller Plaza
New York, NY 10020, USA
Tel.: (212) 636 2000

William Doyle
175 E. 87th Street
New York, NY 10128, USA
Tel.: (212) 427 2730

Sotheby's
34-35, New Bond Street
London W1A 1AA, UK
Tel.: 0207 293 5000

Sotheby's USA
1334, York Avenue at
72nd Street
New York, NY 10021, USA
Tel.: (212) 606 7000

Bibliography

Braun, Peter. Wristwatch Annual. *New York: Abbeville Press, 2001.*

Britten, F.J.J. Watch and Clockmaker's Handbook, Dictionary and Guide. *Woodbridge, UK: Antique Collector's Club, 1996.*

Childers, Caroline. The Master Wristwatches. *New York: BW Publishing, 1999.*

Cologni, Franco. Cartier: The Tank Watch. *Paris: Flammarion, 1998.*

Edwards, Frank. Wristwatches: a Connoisseur's Guide. *Westport, CT: Firefly, 1997.*

Fabern Edward. American Wristwatches: Five Decades of Style and Design. *Atglen, PA: Schiffer Publishing, 1996.*

Kreuzer, Anton. Omega Designs. *Atglen, PA: Schiffer Publishing, 1996.*

Meis, Reinhard. Chronograph Wristwatches: To Stop Time. *Atglen, PA: Schiffer Publishing, 1993.*

Shugart, Cooksey. The Complete Price Guide to Watches. *Cleveland: Collector Books, 2000.*

Terrisse, Sophie. Prestigious Watches. *New York: Rizzoli Intl., 1996.*

Viola, Gerald, and Gisbert Brunner. Time in Gold. *Atglen, PA: Schiffer Publishing, 1997.*

Acknowledgments

The author wishes to express his thanks to the following for their invaluable help, and for so generously opening their stores and collections to us:

Jean-Yves Vergara, Galerie Ouaiss-Hady;
René Bruyeron, Watch Déco;
Eric Hamdi, Montres Modernes et de Collection;
Romain Réa, Explor'heure;
Bernard Tranier, La Pendulerie de Lyon;
Christian Odin, Boutique Crésus;
Jean-Michel Piguet of the International Watch Museum
in Le-Chaux-de-Fonds, Switzerland;
Maria-Pia Coustans;
Daniel Galazzo;
Thierry Huguenin of the French Watch Collector's Club;
Jean-Claude Berton;
Adrien Maeght, a true lover of beautiful objects;
Béatrice Vaccaro, press officer at Ebel Watches;
Isabelle Gervais, press officer at Jaeger-LeCoultre Watches;
Éloïse Caron, press officer at Swatch Watches;
and finally, Claire Ducamp, discreet and efficient s ever.

In the same series

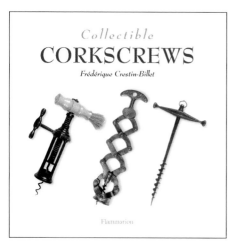

Collectible CORKSCREWS
Frédérique Crestin-Billet

Collectible POCKET KNIVES
Dominique Pascal

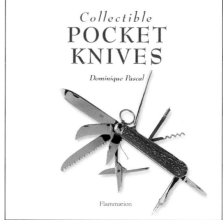

Collectible MINIATURE
PERFUME BOTTLES
Anne Breton

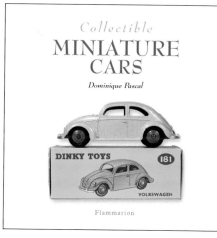

Collectible MINIATURE CARS
Dominique Pascal

Collectible FOUNTAIN PENS
J. M. Clark

Collectible PIPES
Jean Rebeyrolles

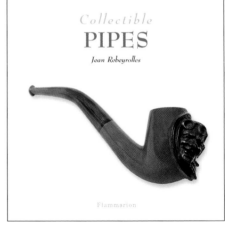

Collectible SNOWDOMES
Lélie Carnot

Photographic Credits

FA0621-02-VI
Dépot légal: 09/2001